SECOND EDITION

TOUCHSTONE

STUDENT'S BOOK 3A

MICHAEL McCARTHY

JEANNE McCARTEN

HELEN SANDIFORD

CAMBRIDGE
UNIVERSITY PRESS

CAMBRIDGE
UNIVERSITY PRESS

University Printing House, Cambridge CB2 8BS, United Kingdom

One Liberty Plaza, 20th Floor, New York, NY 10006, USA

477 Williamstown Road, Port Melbourne, VIC 3207, Australia

314–321, 3rd Floor, Plot 3, Splendor Forum, Jasola District Centre, New Delhi – 110025, India

103 Penang Road, #05-06/07, Visioncrest Commercial, Singapore 238467

Cambridge University Press is part of the University of Cambridge.

It furthers the University's mission by disseminating knowledge in the pursuit of
education, learning and research at the highest international levels of excellence.

www.cambridge.org
Information on this title: www.cambridge.org/9781107628755

First published 2005
Second Edition 2014

40 39 38 37 36 35 34 33 32 31 30 29 28 27 26 25 24 23 22 21

Printed in Malaysia by Vivar Printing

A catalogue record for this publication is available from the British Library

ISBN 978-1-107-66583-5 Student's Book
ISBN 978-1-107-62875-5 Student's Book A
ISBN 978-1-107-69446-0 Student's Book B
ISBN 978-1-107-64271-3 Workbook
ISBN 978-1-107-62082-7 Workbook A
ISBN 978-1-107-65147-0 Workbook B
ISBN 978-1-107-62794-9 Full Contact
ISBN 978-1-107-63739-9 Full Contact A
ISBN 978-1-107-63903-4 Full Contact B
ISBN 978-1-107-68094-4 Teacher's Edition with Assessment Audio CD/CD-ROM
ISBN 978-1-107-63179-3 Class Audio CDs (4)

Additional resources for this publication at www.cambridge.org/touchstone2

Acknowledgments

Touchstone Second Edition has benefited from extensive development research. The authors and publishers would like to extend their thanks to the following reviewers and consultants for their valuable insights and suggestions:

Ana Lúcia da Costa Maia de Almeida and Mônica da Costa Monteiro de Souza from **IBEU**, Rio de Janeiro, Brazil; Andreza Cristiane Melo do Lago from **Magic English School,** Manaus, Brazil; Magaly Mendes Lemos from **ICBEU**, São José dos Campos, Brazil; Maria Lucia Zaorob, São Paulo, Brazil; Patricia McKay Aronis from **CEL LEP**, São Paulo, Brazil; Carlos Gontow, São Paulo, Brazil; Christiane Augusto Gomes da Silva from **Colégio Visconde de Porto Seguro,** São Paulo, Brazil; Silvana Fontana from **Lord's Idiomas**, São Paulo, Brazil; Alexander Fabiano Morishigue from **Speed Up Idiomas**, Jales, Brazil; Elisabeth Blom from **Casa Thomas Jefferson**, Brasília, Brazil; Michelle Dear from **International Academy of English**, Toronto, ON, Canada; Walter Duarte Marin, Laura Hurtado Portela, Jorge Quiroga, and Ricardo Suarez, from **Centro Colombo Americano**, Bogotá, Colombia; Jhon Jairo Castaneda Macias from **Praxis English Academy**, Bucaramanga, Colombia; Gloria Liliana Moreno Vizcaino from **Universidad Santo Tomas**, Bogotá, Colombia; Elizabeth Ortiz from **Copol English Institute (COPEI)**, Guayaquil, Ecuador; Henry Foster from **Kyoto Tachibana University**, Kyoto, Japan; Steven Kirk from **Tokyo University**, Tokyo, Japan; J. Lake from **Fukuoka Woman's University**, Fukuoka, Japan; Etsuko Yoshida from **Mie University**, Mie, Japan; B. Bricklin Zeff from **Hokkai Gakuen University**, Hokkaido, Japan; Ziad Abu-Hamatteh from **Al-Balqa' Applied University**, Al-Salt, Jordan; Roxana Pérez Flores from **Universidad Autonoma de Coahuila Language Center**, Saltillo, Mexico; Kim Alejandro Soriano Jimenez from **Universidad Politecnica de Altamira**, Altamira, Mexico; Tere Calderon Rosas from **Universidad Autonoma Metropolitana Campus Iztapalapa**, Mexico City, Mexico; Lilia Bondareva, Polina Ermakova, and Elena Frumina, from **National Research Technical University MISiS**, Moscow, Russia; Dianne C. Ellis from **Kyung Hee University**, Gyeonggi-do, South Korea; Jason M. Ham and Victoria Jo from **Institute of Foreign Language Education, Catholic University of Korea**, Gyeonggi-do, South Korea; Shaun Manning from **Hankuk University of Foreign Studies**, Seoul, South Korea; Natalie Renton from **Busan National University of Education**, Busan, South Korea; Chris Soutter from **Busan University of Foreign Studies**, Busan, South Korea; Andrew Cook from **Dong A University**, Busan, South Korea; Raymond Wowk from **Daejin University**, Gyeonggi-do, South Korea; Ming-Hui Hsieh and Jessie Huang from **National Central University**, Zhongli, Taiwan; Kim Phillips from **Chinese Culture University**, Taipei, Taiwan; Alex Shih from **China University of Technology**, Taipei Ta-Liao Township, Taiwan; Porntip Bodeepongse from **Thaksin University**, Songkhla, Thailand; Nattaya Puakpong and Pannathon Sangarun from **Suranaree University of Technology**, Nakhon Ratchasima, Thailand; Barbara Richards, Gloria Stewner-Manzanares, and Caroline Thompson, from **Montgomery College**, Rockville, MD, USA; Kerry Vrabel from **Gateway Community College**, Phoenix, AZ, USA.

Touchstone Second Edition authors and publishers would also like to thank the following individuals and institutions who have provided excellent feedback and support on *Touchstone Blended*:

Gordon Lewis, Vice President, Laureate Languages and Chris Johnson, Director, Laureate English Programs, Latin America from **Laureate International Universities; Universidad de las Americas**, Santiago, Chile; **University of Victoria**, Paris, France; **Universidad Technólogica Centroamericana**, Honduras; **Institut Universitaire de Casablanca**, Morocco; **Universidad Peruana de Ciencias Aplicadas**, Lima, Peru; **CIBERTEC**, Peru; **National Research Technical University (MiSIS)**, Moscow, Russia; **Institut Obert de Catalunya (IOC)**, Barcelona, Spain; Sedat Çilingir, Burcu Tezcan, and Didem Mutçalıoğlu from **İstanbul Bilgi Üniversitesi**, Istanbul, Turkey.

Touchstone Second Edition authors and publishers would also like to thank the following contributors to *Touchstone Second Edition*:

Sue Aldcorn, Frances Amrani, Deborah Gordon, Lisa Hutchins, Nancy Jordan, Steven Kirk, Genevieve Kocienda, Linda-Marie Koza, Geraldine Mark, Julianna Nielsen, Kathryn O'Dell, Nicola Prentis, Ellen Shaw, Kristin Sherman, Luis Silva Susa, Mary Vaughn, Kerry S. Vrabel, Shari Young, and Eric Zuarino.

Authors' Acknowledgments

The authors would like to thank all the Cambridge University Press staff and freelancers who were involved in the creation of *Touchstone Second Edition*. In addition, they would like to acknowledge a huge debt of gratitude that they owe to two people: Mary Vaughn, for her role in creating *Touchstone First Edition* and for being a constant source of wisdom ever since, and Bryan Fletcher, who also had the vision that has led to the success of *Touchstone Blended Learning*.

Helen Sandiford would like to thank her family for their love and support, especially her husband Bryan.

The author team would also like to thank each other, for the joy of working together, sharing the same professional dedication, and for the mutual support and friendship.

Finally, the authors would like to thank our dear friend Alejandro Martinez, Global Training Manager, who sadly passed away in 2012. He is greatly missed by all who had the pleasure to work with him. Alex was a huge supporter of *Touchstone* and everyone is deeply grateful to him for his contribution to its success.

Touchstone Level 3A Contents and learning outcomes

	Learning outcomes	Language		
		Grammar	Vocabulary	Pronunciation
Unit 1 The way we are pages 1–10	• Talk about people's behavior using adverbs • Describe people's personalities using adverbs before adjectives • Use *always* with a continuous verb to describe habits • Use *at least* to point out the positive side of a situation • Read online student profiles • Write a personal profile	• Adjectives vs. manner adverbs • Adverbs before adjectives and adverbs • Adjective prefixes ***Extra practice***	• Behavior and personality • Personal qualities	***Speaking naturally*** • Rising and falling intonation in questions giving alternatives ***Sounds right*** • Word stress
Unit 2 Experiences pages 11–20	• Talk about experiences and secret dreams using the present perfect • Ask about unusual experiences using present perfect questions • Keep a conversation going • Show interest with *Do you?, Have you?,* etc. • Read a travel blog • Write a post for a travel blog	• Present perfect statements • Present perfect and simple past questions and answers ***Extra practice***	• Past participles of irregular verbs	***Speaking naturally*** • Reduced and unreduced forms of *have* ***Sounds right*** • Different ways to pronounce the letter *o*
Unit 3 Wonders of the world pages 21–30	• Talk about the best, worst, and most beautiful things in your city and country • Describe natural features • Use short responses to be a supportive listener • Use superlatives for emphasis • Read an article about world records • Write a factual article about your country	• Superlatives • Questions with *How* + adjective . . . ? ***Extra practice***	• Buildings and structures • Natural features	***Speaking naturally*** • Linking and deletion with superlatives ***Sounds right*** • Which sound in each group is different?
Checkpoint Units 1–3 pages 31–32				
Unit 4 Family life pages 33–42	• Talk about family life using *let, make, help, have, get, want, ask,* and *tell* • Talk about your immediate and extended family • Describe memories using *used to* and *would* • Give opinions with expressions like *If you ask me* • Agree with opinions using expressions like *Absolutely* • Read a blog about family meals • Write a blog entry about a family memory	• Verbs *let, make, help, have, get, want, ask,* and *tell* • *Used to* and *would* ***Extra practice***	• Types of families • Relatives and extended family members	***Speaking naturally*** • Reduction of *used to* ***Sounds right*** • Matching vowel sounds
Unit 5 Food choices pages 43–52	• Talk about eating habits using containers and quantities • Talk about different ways to cook food • Talk about food using *too, too much, many,* and *enough* • Respond to suggestions by letting the other person decide • Use expressions like *I'm fine* to politely refuse offers • Read about snacks around the world • Write about a dish from your country	• Review of countable and uncountable nouns • Quantifiers *a little, a few, very little,* and *very few* • *Too, too much, too many,* and *enough* ***Extra practice***	• Containers and quantities • Different ways of cooking food	***Speaking naturally*** • Stressing new information ***Sounds right*** • Are the sounds the same or different?
Unit 6 Managing life pages 53–62	• Talk about future plans and schedules using *will, be going to,* present continuous, and simple present • Ask for and give advice about personal situations using modal verbs and expressions • Use expressions with *make* and *do* • End phone calls with expressions like *I'd better go* • Say good-bye in a friendly, informal way • Read a blog about multitasking • Write some advice about time management	• The future with *will, be going to,* the present continuous, and the simple present • Use *had better, ought to,* and *might want to* to say what's advisable • Use *have to* and *going to have to* to say what's necessary • Use *would rather* to say what's preferable ***Extra practice***	• Expressions with *make* and *do*	***Speaking naturally*** • Reduction of verbs *want to, you'd better, going to have to, ought to,* and *have got to* ***Sounds right*** • Matching vowel sounds
Checkpoint Units 4–6 pages 63–64				

Interaction	Skills				Self study
Conversation strategies	**Listening**	**Reading**	**Writing**	**Free talk**	**Vocabulary notebook**
• Use *always* and a continuous verb to talk about things people do more than is usual • Use *at least* to point out the positive side of a situation	***People I admire most*** • Listen to people talk about people they admire and fill in a chart ***Things you don't know about me*** • Predict what people will say next	***Student profiles*** • Online student profiles	***Your personal profile*** • Write a personal profile • Useful expressions for biographical writing	***What are we like?*** • Class activity: Ask questions to find out new things about your classmates	***Happy or sad?*** • When you learn a new word, find out if it has an opposite
• Keep the conversation going • Use response questions like *Do you?* and *Have you?* to show interest	***What have they done?*** • Listen to conversations about things people have done and choose the best responses ***A traveler's adventures*** • Listen to a conversation about travel and identify information; then answer questions about details	***Travel blogs*** • Read travel blogs	***Blog about it*** • Write a blog entry about an exciting experience • Use adverbs like *fortunately*, *unfortunately*, and *amazingly* to show your attitude or feeling	***I've never done that!*** • Group game: Play a game to find out things that your classmates have never done	***Have you ever . . . ?*** • When you learn a new verb, write the three main forms in a chart
• Use short responses with *really* and *sure* to agree and be a supportive listener • Use superlatives to emphasize your opinions and feelings	***What do you know?*** • Listen to a quiz and answer questions ***Travel talk*** • Listen to an interview about travel experiences and answer questions	***World records*** • Read an article about world records	***Interesting facts*** • Write a paragraph about an interesting place in your country • Adding information	***Where's the best place to . . . ?*** • Pair work: Think of advice to give to someone visiting your country for the first time	***From the mountains to the sea*** • Draw a map of your country and label it

Checkpoint Units 1–3   pages 31–32

• Give opinions with expressions like *It seems like . . .* and *If you ask me, . . .* • Use expressions like *exactly*, *definitely*, and *absolutely* to agree with people's opinions	***Reasonable demands?*** • Listen to people talk about demands their parents make on them ***Family memories*** • Listen to people talk about things they used to do	***Barbara's Blog*** • Read a blog about family meals	***Family memories*** • Write a blog about a family memory • Time markers to show the past and present	***Family histories*** • Group work: Prepare a short history of your family and share it with your group	***Remember that?*** • Use word webs to log new vocabulary about your family members
• Respond to suggestions by letting the other person decide • Refuse offers politely with expressions like *No, thanks. I'm fine.*	***That sounds good.*** • Listen to conversations and number pictures in order; then match each picture with the best response ***Snack habits*** • Listen to people talk about snacks and fill in a chart	***Snacks around the world*** • Read an article about popular snacks from around the world	***You should definitely try it!*** • Write an article about a popular snack from your country • Give examples with *like*, *for example*, and *such as*	***Whichever is easier*** • Group work: Plan a "pot luck" dinner with your group	***Fried bananas*** • Learn new words in combination with other words
• End phone conversations with expressions like *I'd better go*, *I've got to go*, and *I'll call you later* • Use informal expressions like *See you later* to end friendly phone conversations	***Fun invitations*** • Listen to three people respond to different invitations and fill in a chart ***When should I do that?*** • Listen to four people talk about their time management problems and identify how they solved them	***The art (and science) of doing less and achieving more*** • Read an article about multitasking	***When should I do that?*** • Write advice about time management • Link ideas using *as long as*, *provided that*, and *unless*	***Who's going to do what?*** • Group work: Plan a community event and tell the class about your event	***Do your best!*** • When you learn a new expression, use it in a sentence to help you remember it

Checkpoint Units 4–6   pages 63–64

Useful language for . . .

Working in groups

Does anyone else have anything to add?

What do you think, _____?

Let's take turns asking the questions. OK, who wants to go first?

Do you want me to make the list?

Should I write down the information this time?

Do you have any ideas?

Do you know what the answer is?

We're going to do a role play about . . .

In our survey, we found out that . . .

We agreed on these things. First, . . .

We're finished. What should we do next?

Checking your partner's work

Can you help me with this question? I'm stuck.

I can't figure out this answer. Can you help me?

Would you mind checking my work?

Let's compare answers.

Let's exchange papers.

I can't read your writing. What does this say?

I'm not sure what you mean. Do you mean _____?

I don't understand what this means. Are you trying to say _____?

Your blog was really interesting. I just wanted to ask you a question about _____.

I was wondering about _____.

The way we are

 Can Do! In this unit, you learn how to . . .

Lesson A
- Talk about people's behavior using manner adverbs and adjectives

Lesson B
- Describe people's personalities using adverbs like *extremely* before adjectives

Lesson C
- Use *always* with a continuous verb to describe habits
- Use *at least* to point out the positive side of a situation

Lesson D
- Read online student profiles
- Write a personal profile

Before you begin . . .

Who looks outgoing? shy? stylish? conservative?
Which people would you like to meet? Why?

Do you need to slow down?

Take this quiz to find out.

1

When I walk down the street, . . .

a I walk very fast and use the time to make phone calls.

b I enjoy the walk and look at the things and people around me.

2

When I go out to lunch with friends, . . .

a I eat quickly so that I can get back to my work.

b I eat slowly, and I enjoy the food and conversation.

3

When there's a family event, . . .

a I often have to miss it because I have too much to do.

b I try to plan my time well so that I can attend the event.

4

If traffic is heavy and some people are driving a bit recklessly, . . .

a I honk my horn a lot. I get mad easily in bad traffic.

b I automatically slow down and try to drive carefully.

5

If I'm waiting at the airport and find out that my flight is delayed, . . .

a I get impatient and complain to the people behind the counter.

b I wait patiently. I read something or make a few phone calls.

6

If I'm in a hurry and think people are talking too slowly, . . .

a I sometimes interrupt them to finish their sentences.

b I listen quietly and wait for them to finish before I talk.

7

If I play a game or sport with friends, . . .

a I take the game seriously, and I feel very bad if I lose.

b I think it's better to win than lose, but I don't feel strongly about it.

8

If I get an assignment with a very tight deadline, . . .

a I get very stressed – I hate it when I don't have time to do a job properly.

b I work hard to do the best I can in the time I have.

Mostly A answers?

It's time to slow down and enjoy life more. Try to plan your time differently. Make more time for family, friends, and fun.

Mostly B answers?

You're balancing work and play nicely. Just keep the balance right.

1 Getting started

A Are you ever in a hurry? When? Tell the class.

"I'm usually in a hurry in the mornings when I have to get ready for class."

B 1.02 Listen and take the quiz above. For each item, circle *a* or *b*.

C Pair work Compare your quiz responses with a partner. How are you alike? different?

D Circle the correct words. Use the quiz to help you. Then tell a partner which sentences are true for you.

1. I have a lot of **tight / tightly** deadlines.
2. I plan my time **good / well**.
3. I often eat lunch **quick / quickly**.
4. I feel **strong / strongly** about my opinions.
5. I get **impatient / impatiently** in long lines.
6. I work **hard / hardly** to get good grades.

2 Grammar Adjectives vs. manner adverbs ◀)) 1.03

Extra practice p. 140

Adjective + noun
I'm a **patient** person.
He's not a **good** singer.
He's a **fast** driver.
She's a **careful** driver.

Regular -ly adverbs
patient ▶ patient**ly**
careful ▶ careful**ly**
easy ▶ eas**ily**
automatic ▶ automatic**ally**

Verb + manner adverb
I wait **patiently** in lines.
He doesn't sing very **well**.
He drives very **fast**.
She drives **carefully**.

Irregular adverbs
good ▶ **well**
late ▶ **late**
fast ▶ **fast**
hard ▶ **hard**

***be, feel, get*, etc., + adjective**
I'm **patient**.
His voice **sounds terrible**.
He **gets reckless** sometimes.
I **feel safe*** with her.
***But:** I **feel strongly** about it.

In conversation
The most common *-ly* manner adverbs are *quickly, easily, differently, automatically, slowly, properly, badly, strongly,* and *carefully.*

✕ Common errors
Don't use an adjective to describe how someone does an action.
*Children learn languages **easily**.*
(NOT *Children learn languages easy.*)

A Complete these opinions with the correct forms of the words given.

1. Young people talk really ___*fast*___ (fast) and don't speak _____ (clear). And they use a lot of slang. It sounds _____ (terrible). They don't always communicate _____ (good).

2. People aren't very _____ (patient) when they have to wait in long lines. They don't speak to the clerks very _____ (polite), either.

3. Sometimes families argue because parents and children see things _____ (different).

4. A lot of people _____ (automatic) answer their cell phones when they ring, even at dinner. I think that's just _____ (rude).

5. People don't feel _____ (safe) on the roads because so many people are driving _____ (reckless). Driving can be _____ (dangerous).

6. A lot of people try _____ (hard) to do their job _____ (careful) and _____ (thorough) and they get stressed.

About you B Pair work Discuss the opinions. Are they true in your culture?

"People here talk very fast so you have to listen carefully."

3 Speaking naturally Questions giving alternatives

Are you usually on time for **class**? Or do you often arrive **late**?

A ◀)) 1.04 Listen and repeat the questions above. Notice how the intonation rises in the first question and falls in the second question.

About you B ◀)) 1.05 Now listen and repeat these questions. Then ask and answer the questions with a partner.

1. Do you do homework assignments carefully? Or do you just do them quickly?
2. Do you learn new English words easily? Or do you have to work hard at it?
3. Do you usually do well on tests? Or do you just get passing grades?
4. Do you practice English regularly outside of class? Or do you just use it in class?
5. Do you see things differently from your classmates? Or do you share their opinions?
6. Do you listen to class announcements carefully? Or do you ignore them?

1 Building vocabulary and grammar

A 🔊 1.06 Listen and read. Who do these people admire? Why?

Who is someone you really admire?

"My English teacher. She's incredibly **talented** and **creative**. And she **has a great sense of humor**. She's pretty **disorganized**, though. She forgets something almost every class, but her classes are absolutely wonderful!"

– Jessica Davis

"I really admire a guy in my karate class. He's extremely **competitive**, but when he wins, he's not **arrogant** like some of the other guys. He's not very **outgoing**, so some people think he's **unfriendly**, but I think he's basically just **shy**."

– Mike Kowalski

"I think my dad's a pretty cool guy. We get along really well. He's fairly **easygoing** and **laid-back**. And he's very **practical** and **down-to-earth**, so he always gives me good advice. Also, he's completely **honest** with me. I can trust what he says."

– Bryan Yuen

"My friend Luisa. She's so **helpful** and **generous**. I mean, she's always doing things for other people. She's not **selfish** at all. And she's totally **reliable**. If she says she'll help you with something, she does. You can always count on her."

– Emilia Perez

Word sort **B** Which of the personality words or expressions above describe these qualities? Do you know any people with these qualities? Compare with a partner.

Winning is very important to you.	*competitive*	You're relaxed about life.	
You handle small problems well.		You never cheat or steal.	
People can always count on you.		You're not well organized.	
You don't get along with people.		You can do lot of things well.	
You like to have fun with people.		You think you're the best.	
You're not relaxed around people.		You give a lot of time or money.	

Figure it out **C** Find words in the article that make these adjectives stronger.

📓 **Vocabulary notebook** p. 10

1. _incredibly_ talented
2. _____ practical
3. _____ disorganized
4. _____ honest
5. _____ competitive
6. _____ reliable

Figure it out **D** Find words in the article that have the opposite meaning.

1. friendly _____
2. organized _____
3. unreliable _____

2 **Grammar** Adverbs before adjectives and adverbs ◀))) 1.07

Extra practice p. 140

Use *incredibly, extremely, very, really,* and *so* to make some adjectives and adverbs stronger.

She's **incredibly** talented.
She's **extremely** generous.
He's a **really** cool guy.
We get along **very** well.

Use *pretty* and *fairly* to mean "more than a little."

He's **pretty** easygoing.
He's **fairly** laid-back.

Use *absolutely* or *really* (but not *very*) with adjectives that are already very strong.

She's **absolutely** wonderful.
He's **really** fantastic.

The expression *at all* makes negatives stronger.

She's **not** selfish **at all**.

Completely and *totally* mean 100%.

He's **completely** honest.
She's **totally** reliable.

Adjective prefixes
patient ▶ **im**patient
considerate ▶ **in**considerate
friendly ▶ **un**friendly
reliable ▶ **un**reliable
honest ▶ **dis**honest
organized ▶ **dis**organized

In conversation

People use *really* and *pretty* much more often in conversation than in writing.

really
pretty

conversation ■ : ■ writing

A Do you know people with these qualities? Write a sentence for each expression. Add an example.

1. totally laid-back
2. pretty generous
3. very honest
4. absolutely wonderful
5. not competitive at all
6. incredibly impatient
7. fairly disorganized
8. completely reliable
9. extremely talented
10. really inconsiderate

B **Pair work** Compare sentences with a partner.

A *My boyfriend is totally laid-back. He always goes along with my plans and everything.*
B *Really? He sounds incredibly easygoing.*

3 **Listening and speaking** People I admire most

A ◀))) 1.08 Listen. Who do these people admire? Write the people in the chart.

	John	Marina	Hiroyuki
1. Who do you admire?			
2. Why?			
3. What do you have in common?			
4. How are you different?			

B ◀))) 1.08 Listen again. What do they say about the people they admire?

C **Pair work** Ask and answer the questions. Then join another pair. Tell them about the person your partner admires.

A *Who do you admire?*
B *I admire my sister. She's extremely friendly and totally reliable. She . . .*

Sounds right p. 137

5

1 Conversation strategy Describing individual habits

A Which two habits do you think are most annoying in a co-worker or classmate? Tell the class.

Someone who . . .

☐ smiles all the time ☐ criticizes others ☐ stands around and talks
☐ disturbs people ☐ wastes time ☐ talks about people behind their backs

B ◀)) 1.09 **Listen. What's Ellie's new co-worker like? How is he different from her last co-worker?**

Max	Hey, how are you getting along with your new co-worker? He seems extremely friendly. He's always smiling.
Ellie	You mean Jim? Well, yeah, he is, but he never does any work. He's always disturbing people. It drives me crazy. You know, he's always standing around and talking.
Max	Well, at least he's pleasant.
Ellie	Yeah. And he's not always criticizing people like that last guy.
Max	Yeah. He was pretty bad. He was always talking about people behind their backs.
Ellie	I mean, at least Jim's not like that. But like, he's always wasting time.
Max	You mean like we're doing right now?

C Notice how Ellie and Max use *always* and a continuous verb to talk about things people do a lot or more than is usual. Find other examples in the conversation.

"He's always wasting time."

D Change the underlined parts of these sentences to describe habits. Use *always* and a continuous verb. Compare with a partner.

1. I'm pretty disorganized. I <u>lose</u> things. *I'm always losing things.*
2. Everyone in my family loves music. We <u>sing</u> together.
3. My brother is really generous with his time. He <u>fixes</u> my computer.
4. My father is a workaholic. He <u>comes</u> home late. And he <u>brings</u> work home with him, too.
5. My college roommate was really funny. She <u>made</u> us laugh. You know, she <u>told</u> jokes.
6. A friend of mine <u>complains</u> she's broke, but she <u>buys</u> herself expensive clothes.
7. One of my friends is totally unreliable. He <u>cancels</u> plans at the last minute.

About you E Pair work Do you know people like the ones above? Tell a partner.

"My sister is pretty disorganized. She's always losing her keys."

2 Strategy plus *At least*

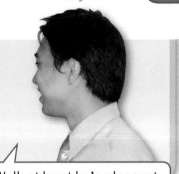

You can use the expression *at least* to point out the positive side of a situation.

 In conversation

At least is one of the top 500 words and expressions.

He's always standing around and talking.

Well, at least he's pleasant.

🔊 **1.10** Add *at least* to each comment. Listen and check. Do you know anyone like these people? Tell a partner.

1. My girlfriend's always running behind, but she calls to say she'll be late.
2. My best friend is always borrowing my clothes. She returns them in good condition.
3. One of my classmates talks about himself a lot. His stories are always interesting.
4. My roommate sleeps all the time, but she doesn't snore. Thank goodness!
5. My parents and I see things differently. We don't have big fights or anything.

   A *My dad's always running behind, but at least he says he's sorry when he's late.*

   B *Well, my friend is always telling me I'm late, so . . .*

3 Strategies *Funny little habits*

A 🔊 **1.11** Complete each conversation with *always* and a continuous verb. Add *at least* to each response. Then listen and check.

1. A My boyfriend _____ (check) his messages, even at the movies!

   B Oh, that's annoying. But he doesn't answer his phone during a movie, right?

2. A My girlfriend _____ (tell) jokes. She never takes anything seriously.

   B Well, she has a good sense of humor.

3. A Sometimes I'm so disorganized. I _____ (lose) things, like pens and stuff.

   B Yeah, but you don't lose anything really valuable, right?

4. A My sister _____ (ask) me for money. She asks nicely, so it's hard to say no.

   B Well, she asks politely.

B **Pair work** Practice the conversations above with a partner.

About you C **Pair work** Talk about people with habits like these. Think of something positive to say.

- texting
- chewing gum
- falling asleep in class
- singing or whistling
- forgetting things
- telling jokes
- losing things
- looking in mirrors
- daydreaming

"*My friend is always texting, but at least she doesn't do it while she's crossing the street.*"

1 Reading

A Think of two questions you would ask a new classmate. Tell the class.

B Read the profiles. Who would you like to meet? Why?

 http://www.onlineenglishclass... Q

STUDENT PROFILES Meet your classmates in our online English class.

1. MARIANA BARELLI MATOS

What's your major? Fashion design. My dream is to create incredibly beautiful clothes for women all over the world.

Where are you based? In Milan. I was born and raised in São Paulo, Brazil, but my mother's Italian. She felt very strongly that I should experience her culture.

Why did you choose your major? I inherited my mother's love of fashion. She's very style-conscious and has impeccable taste in clothes.

What skills do you have? I speak Portuguese and Italian fluently and have some knowledge of Mandarin.

What do you do in your free time? I love the outdoors, and I'm fairly adventurous. During the summers I volunteer at a camp for disadvantaged children. It's extremely rewarding.

3. KATYA AKILOVA

Where are you based? In Moscow, Russia, though I'm from St. Petersburg, originally.

What do your friends say about you? That I'm very down-to-earth, hard-working, and incredibly organized, and that I'm always setting goals for myself.

What's your worst habit? I'm always doing something. I find it hard to relax.

What are your future plans? As a science major, I'm considering a career as an environmentalist because I feel strongly about protecting the environment.

What skills do you have? I'm an accomplished accordion player. I started playing at the age of eight. I'd love to play professionally with an orchestra.

2. MATEO REYES

Where are you from? I was born and raised in Veracruz, Mexico.

What do your friends say about you? They say that I'm extremely laid-back and even-tempered. And that I'm too humble about my talents.

What are your future plans? I have so many. Right now I'm working for a small production company called Film Fast. My major was film studies, and my goal is to tell real-life stories creatively through television and film.

What do you do in your free time? I like to cook, and I'm always trying out new recipes, especially for desserts.

What's something people don't know about you? When I was 12, I was on a reality TV show for young chefs. I didn't win, but at least I tried.

4. AHMED ABD EL-SALAM

What's your job? I'm an engineer. I work for a big company called Syntix.

Why did you choose to study online? You get to "meet" an incredibly diverse range of students, and the teachers are extremely supportive. I can be pretty shy and introverted and studying online feels safe somehow.

Do you have a secret talent? I play guitar in a band called All Kinds. We play all kinds of music. I feel like a totally different person in the band – outgoing and not shy at all.

What are your tips for new students? Take your studies seriously. Make the most of your opportunities to practice English with other students.

C Answer the questions about the students in the profiles. Which student (or students) . . .

- enjoys playing music?
- is very hard-working?
- already has a job?
- is an outdoor type?
- is very serious?
- wants a creative career?
- seems like fun?

D Find the adjectives on the left in the student profiles, and guess their meaning.
Then circle the best options to explain them.

1. experience   I should **have contact with** / **ignore** my mother's culture.
2. disadvantaged   The children are **poor** / **rich**.
3. humble   I **think** / **don't think** I am really good at things.
4. considering   This is something I **am** / **am not** thinking about.
5. diverse   The students are all **the same** / **different**.
6. introverted   I'm **very outgoing** / **not outgoing at all**.

About you **E** **Pair work** Ask and answer the questions in the profiles. Give your own answers.

[2] Listening Things you don't know about me

A 🔊 1.12 Listen to five people talk about themselves. Match the people and the things they will
probably say next.

Name	Something you don't know about me
1. Ana	_____ I can play two instruments really well.
2. Kevin	_____ I'm a pretty good cook.
3. Jen	_*Ana*_ I'm a fairly good singer.
4. Patrick	_____ I'm extremely allergic to nuts.
5. Tom	_____ I speak two languages fluently.

B 🔊 1.12 Listen again. Write three pieces of information about each person above. Compare with a
partner. Did you write the same facts?

1. Ana started lessons in elementary school.

[3] Writing and speaking Your personal profile

About you **A** Write a profile about yourself. Choose five questions from the student profiles, and include
information that other people don't know about you. Don't write your name.

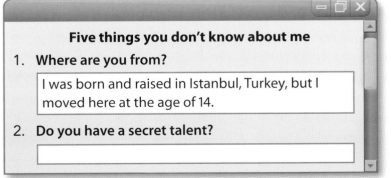

Five things you don't know about me
1. **Where are you from?**

I was born and raised in Istanbul, Turkey, but I
moved here at the age of 14.

2. **Do you have a secret talent?**

Help note

Useful expressions

I **was born and raised in** . . .
At the age of 17, I . . .
I **can be** . . .
I work for a company **called** . . .
I'm an **accomplished** . . .
I **started playing** the flute . . .

B **Class activity** Mix up all the profiles. Select one and guess who wrote it.
Tell the class. Were you right?

Free talk p. 129

Vocabulary notebook / Happy or sad?

Learning tip *Learning opposite meanings*

When you learn a new word, find out if it has an "opposite." Be careful – sometimes a word has different meanings and different opposites.

This exercise is hard.	≠	*This exercise is easy.*
He's a hard worker.	≠	*He's lazy. He doesn't work hard.*
This chair feels hard.	≠	*This chair feels soft.*

In conversation

Adjectives without prefixes are much more frequent in conversation.

```
████████████ happy
██ unhappy
███████████████ honest
██ dishonest
```

1 Rewrite the sentences so that they have an opposite meaning. Use the words in the box.

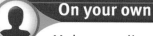

happy   polite   mean   well

1. My father drives really badly.
2. My best friend can be very kind.

3. My boss is an extremely rude person.
4. I was pretty unhappy in school.

2 For each of the underlined words, think of a word with an opposite meaning.

1. I have a pretty <u>loud</u> voice.
2. My classmate is extremely <u>outgoing</u>.
3. I'm usually <u>late</u> for appointments.

4. My brother eats very <u>slowly</u>.
5. I think English is <u>difficult</u>.
6. My sister and I have <u>different</u> tastes.

3 Word builder Use the prefixes *im-*, *in-*, *un-*, and *dis-* to create opposite meanings for these words.

1. He's **patient**. *impatient*
2. She's **honest**. _____
3. He's **friendly**. _____

4. He's **competent**. _____
5. They're **organized**. _____
6. He looks **healthy**. _____

7. She's **reliable**. _____
8. She's **considerate**. _____

 On your own

Make an online photo book. Write five things about each person's personality and a sentence about any funny little habits they have.

She's extremely funny. She's always telling jokes and laughing.

✔ Can Do! Now I can . . .

✔ I can . . .   ? I need to review how to . . .

- ☐ talk about how people do things.
- ☐ describe people's personalities.
- ☐ make descriptions stronger.
- ☐ use *always* + continuous verb to say what people do a lot.

- ☐ use *at least* to point out positive things.
- ☐ understand people talking about people they admire.
- ☐ predict what people will say next.
- ☐ read online student profiles.
- ☐ write a personal profile.

10

Experiences

✓ Can Do! In this unit, you learn how to . . .

Lesson A
- Talk about experiences and secret dreams using the present perfect

Lesson B
- Ask about unusual experiences using present perfect questions

Lesson C
- Keep a conversation going
- Use *Do you?*, *Have you?*, etc. to show interest

Lesson D
- Read a travel blog
- Write a post for a travel blog

1

2

3

4

Before you begin . . .

Think of some special experiences you hope to have in the future. Tell the class . . .

- a place you'd like to go someday.
- something you'd love to see.
- something you'd like to do.
- a person you'd really like to meet.

11

WE ASKED FIVE PEOPLE,

"What's your secret dream?"

"Actually, I've always wanted to be an actor. I haven't had any formal training, but I've been in a couple of college plays. So my dream is to study acting."

– Jill Richardson
Vancouver, Canada

"Well, Carlos and I have gone sailing a few times with friends, and we've had a lot of fun. So our dream is to buy our own sailboat. But we haven't saved enough money!"

– Sonia and Carlos Silva
Brasília, Brazil

"My dream? To go surfing. I've never tried it before, but my brother goes surfing all the time! He's even surfed in Hawai'i."

– Raquel Garza
Monterrey, Mexico

"Well, my parents have never traveled outside of Japan, so I want to take them to Europe. I've been there many times, so I know all the best places to go!"

– Hiro Tanaka
Osaka, Japan

1 Getting started

A What kinds of hopes and dreams do people have? Make a class list.

"Some people want to go traveling or meet their favorite pop star. . . ."

B ◀)) 1.13 Listen. What is each person's secret dream? Do you have any secret dreams like these?

Figure it out **C** How do the people above express these ideas? Find what they say and underline the verbs.

1. **Jill** I always wanted to be an actor as a child. I want to be an actor now.
2. **Sonia** We didn't save enough money last year. We don't have enough money now.
3. **Raquel** My brother even surfed in Hawai'i — exactly when isn't important.
4. **Hiro** In the past, I went to Europe many times.

2 Grammar Present perfect statements 🔊 1.14

Extra practice p. 141

Use the present perfect for events at an indefinite time before now.

I **'ve been** to Europe.	I **haven't been** to Paris.
You **'ve done** a lot of things	You **haven't gone** sailing.
We **'ve had** a lot of fun.	We **haven't saved** enough money.
They **'ve traveled** in Asia.	They **haven't been** to Europe.
He **'s surfed** in Hawai'i.	She **hasn't tried** surfing before.

The present perfect is often used with these frequency expressions.

I**'ve always wanted** to study acting.
We**'ve gone** sailing **once** / **twice** / **many times**.
She**'s never tried** it **before**.

Notice how people use *been* and *gone* to talk about travel destinations.

I**'ve been** to Paris. (I went and came back.)
She**'s gone** to Paris. (She's still in Paris.)

Regular past participles

travel	traveled	**traveled**
want	wanted	**wanted**
save	saved	**saved**
try	tried	**tried**

Irregular past participles

be	was / were	**been**
do	did	**done**
go	went	**gone**
have	had	**had**
see	saw	**seen**

✗ Common errors

Use the past participle, not the base form.

I've traveled a lot.
(NOT *I've travel a lot.*)

A Complete the conversations with the present perfect. Then practice with a partner.

1. A I *'ve always wanted* (always / want) to try rock climbing.

   B Really? Not me. I _____ (never / want) to do it. I _____ (always / be) afraid of heights.

2. A I _____ (not see) the Grand Canyon. I really want to go there someday.

   B Me too. My friend _____ (be) there. She had an amazing time.

3. A I _____ (go) surfing three or four times. It's exciting.

   B Yeah? I _____ (not try) it before. I _____ (never do) any water sports.

4. A My dream is to be a tennis player. I _____ (have) a lot of training, and I _____ (play) with some professional tennis players.

   B No way! I love tennis. I _____ (always / want) to meet Andy Murray.

5. A We _____ (not travel) much, but we want to go to Bogotá.

   B Me too. My cousin lives there. He _____ (invite) me to visit several times, but I _____ (not save) enough money to go.

About you **B** Pair work Start conversations like the ones above using your own ideas.

"I've always wanted to try hang gliding."   *"Really? My friend's been hang gliding."*

3 Talk about it What are your secret dreams?

Group work Talk about these things. Why haven't you done them? What has stopped you?

▶ something you've always wanted to buy

▶ a place that you've never been to but would like to visit

▶ something you've always wanted to learn how to do

▶ something else you've always wanted to do

1 Building language

A 🔊 1.15 Listen. Which experience do you think was scarier?

HAVE YOU EVER DONE ANYTHING **SCARY**?

"Yes, I have. I went white-water rafting in Ecuador last year, and I fell off the raft. Luckily, my friends pulled me out of the river. But I've never been so scared in my life."
– Mei-ling Chen, Taipei, Taiwan

"No, I haven't. Well, maybe once. I entered a talent contest a couple of years ago and sang in front of a hundred people. That was scary. But I won third place!"
– Martín Suárez, Caracas, Venezuela

Figure it out **B** Unscramble the questions and complete the answers. Then practice with a partner.

1. A to Ecuador / you / been / Have / ever / ?

   B Yes, I _____ . I _____ there last year.

2. A entered / you / Have / a / talent contest / ever / ?

   B No, I _____ . But I _____ in a concert in May.

2 Grammar Present perfect vs. simple past 🔊 1.16

Extra practice p. 141

Use the **present perfect** for indefinite times before now.	**Have** you ever **gone** white-water rafting? No, I **haven't**. I've never **gone** rafting. Yes, I **have**. I **went** rafting **last May**.
Use the **simple past** for specific events or times in the past.	**Did** you **have** a good time? Yes, I **did**. But I **fell** off the raft.

💬 **In conversation**

The most common questions with the present perfect are *Have you (ever) seen / been / heard / had . . . ?*

A Complete the conversations with the present perfect or simple past. Then practice.

1. A _____ you ever _____ (hear) of kitesurfing?

   B Yes, I _____ . But I _____ (never / do) anything like that.

2. A _____ you and your friends ever _____ (go) on a big roller coaster?

   B No, we _____ . I _____ always _____ (hate) roller coasters.

3. A _____ you ever _____ (stay) up all night?

   B Yes, I _____ . My family _____ (go) camping two years ago, and none of us _____ (sleep) all night.

4. A _____ you _____ (do) anything different last summer?

   B Yes, I _____ . I _____ (learn) to play African drums. I _____ always _____ (want) to play them. I _____ (never / go) to Africa, though.

About you **B** Pair work Ask the questions above. Give your own answers.

③ Building vocabulary

About you **A** Ask your classmates about these good and bad experiences. For each question, find someone who answers yes. Write the student's name in the chart.

Good experiences		Bad experiences	
Have you ever . . .	**Name**	**Have you ever . . .**	**Name**
won a prize?		**broken** something valuable?	
gotten 100% on a test?		**lost** something important?	
spoken to a famous person?		**had** the flu?	
taken an exciting trip?		**forgotten** someone's birthday?	
found a wallet?		**fallen** and **hurt** yourself?	

"Have you ever won a prize?"   *"Yes, I have. I won a prize in a science fair in fifth grade."*

Word sort **B** Complete the verb chart. Make another chart with more verbs that you know.

Base form	win			find			fall	
Simple past	*won*	got		took		lost		forgot	hurt
Past participle	*won*		spoken			had		

Vocabulary notebook p. 20

④ Speaking naturally Reduced and unreduced forms of *have*

> A ***Have*** *you ever been to Mexico?*
> B *No, I* ***haven't***. *But my parents* ***have*** *been there several times. (parents**'ve**)*

A ◀)) 1.17 Listen and repeat the question and answer above. Notice how *have* is reduced in questions and full statements but not in short answers.

About you **B** ◀)) 1.18 Listen and complete the questions below. Then ask and answer the questions with a partner. If you answer yes, give a specific example.

1. Have you ever gone <u>*bungee jumping*</u> ?
2. Have you ever been to a _____ ?
3. Have you ever seen a _____ ?
4. Have you ever taken a _____ class?
5. Have you ever had _____ food?
6. Have you ever won a _____ ?
7. Have you ever forgotten an _____ ?
8. Have you ever broken _____ ?

About you **C** **Pair work** Ask the questions above again, this time using your own ideas.

> A *Have you ever gone bungee jumping?*
> B *Actually, I have. I was terrified. I never did it again!*

(((**Sounds right** p. 137

1 Conversation strategy Keeping the conversation going

A What kinds of fun things do people do on the weekends?
Make a list.

B 🔊 1.19 Listen. What fun things has Jason done lately?

Lea	Have you done anything fun lately?
Jason	Yeah, we went to a new club called Fizz last week. Have you been there?
Lea	No, but I've heard good things about it. How was it?
Jason	Yeah, it's neat. The DJ was really good. Do you like techno music?
Lea	Yeah, it's OK, um, not my favorite. I prefer hip-hop.
Jason	Do you? Have you seen that new movie about hip-hop artists?
Lea	No. Is it good?
Jason	Yeah. I've seen it a couple of times.
Lea	Have you? Well, I'm kind of in the mood for a movie. Do you want to see it again?
Jason	Well, I enjoyed it, but . . . I've never seen a movie *three* times!

C Notice how Lea and Jason keep the conversation going.
They say things like *I've heard good things about it* to show
interest and then ask a question. Find other examples in
the conversation.

"Have you been there?"

"No, but I've heard good things about it. How was it?"

D Match each statement with a response. Then practice with a partner.

1. I just saw *Hereafter*. It was a good movie.
   Have you ever seen it? _____

2. Have you ever eaten a lychee? _____

3. I heard a really good band called Sunset recently.
   Do you know them? _____

4. One of my favorite restaurants is Spice House.
   Have you ever eaten there? _____

a. It's a fruit, right? I've never tried one.
   What do they taste like?

b. No, but I've walked by it. What kind of
   food do they serve?

c. No, but I've heard good things about
   them. What kind of music do they play?

d. No, but I've heard of it. What's it about?

About you **E Pair work** Practice the conversations above using your own ideas. Change the underlined words.

2 Strategy plus Response questions

You can show interest by responding with short questions like *Do you?* and *Have you?* Use the same tense as the other person.

In conversation

To show surprise, you can respond with questions like *You do?* and *You have?* This is more informal.

I've seen it a couple of times.

Have you?

Complete the conversations with response questions like *Do you? Are you? Did you?* or *Have you?* Then practice with a partner.

1. A I've never been up in a hot air balloon. I'm afraid of heights.

   B _____ ? Me too. I hate flying.

   A _____ ? I'm the same way. I get sick on airplanes, too.

2. A Have you ever performed in front of an audience?

   B Yes, I have. Actually, I do it all the time.

   A _____ ? Wow.

   B Yeah. I'm a drummer in a rock band.

   A _____ ? I'm impressed!

3. A Have you seen any good movies lately?

   B Actually, I went to see that new action movie that's out right now.

   A _____ ? The one with Liam Neeson? I've seen all his movies.

   B _____ ? So is he your favorite actor?

3 Listening and strategies What have they done?

A ◀)) 1.20 Listen to three people talk about things they have done. Match the people and the main topic they talk about. There are three extra.

1. Albert _____   a. a job   d. a hobby
2. Reny _____   b. vacations   e. a movie on TV
3. Melissa _____   c. a sport   f. an accident

B ◀)) 1.20 Listen again. What did each person just do? Write a sentence.

C ◀)) 1.20 Listen again. Respond to the last thing each person says. Check (✓) the correct response. Then write a question to keep each conversation going.

1. Albert   ☐ *You have?*   ☐ *Did you?*   ☐ *Were you?*   _____
2. Reny   ☐ *Did you?*   ☐ *You were?*   ☐ *You have?*   _____
3. Melissa   ☐ *You did?*   ☐ *Are you?*   ☐ *Do you?*   _____

Free talk p. 129

17

1 Reading

A Look at the photographs. Which trip would you like to take? Tell the class. Then read the two blogs. Which blogger had the worst problems?

`http://www.myblogguatemala...` 🔍

JAKE'S JOURNEY

MARCH 2   GUATEMALA

When we arrived in Guatemala two weeks ago, we didn't know what to expect. But I have to say, we've had a great time. I've done a lot of traveling, and I think it's one of the most amazing places I've ever been to. We've done a lot in the last two weeks. We've gone hiking, explored some of the ancient Mayan ruins, and camped next to a volcano. We've also seen some beautiful birds. The quetzals are so colorful, and there are hummingbirds everywhere. There are lots of things we haven't had time to do. I've always wanted to go to the rain forest. I hope we get there.

Camping was really fun. We drove up some rough dirt roads to Ipala Volcano and got a flat tire on the way. It was worth the trip, though. There's a really pretty lake up there that we hiked around. It rained really hard one night, and everything outside the tent got soaked, but at least the tent didn't leak. Fortunately, the weather's gotten better. Another place we found had these beautiful hot springs and a hot waterfall. Standing underneath it was just like taking a hot shower! I miss you all!

Comments

Linh: You do? That's hard to believe, Jake. It sounds like you're having a blast! I've never been to Central America, but I've always wanted to go there. Have you gone on one of the zip lines? I've heard you can do them there. Have fun!

`http://www.myblogbrazil...` 🔍

CHLOE'S TRAVELS

March 2   Brazil

After 36 hours of travel, we arrived in Brazil last Sunday. I can't believe it – we got stuck on our way here, and unfortunately, we missed Carnival in Rio! I've always wanted to see it – with all the costumes and dancing and music, but we just couldn't get here in time. And I lost my camera!

Fortunately, I've been good about uploading all my photos to the blog, so I haven't lost many. At least it wasn't an expensive camera. Anyway, we've been to the beach every day. We've gone surfing, and I went parasailing yesterday. The views were amazing!

We've done a lot of sightseeing – though we haven't taken the cable car up Sugar Loaf Mountain. We'll probably do that tomorrow. We've met some really nice people. They're so incredibly friendly and helpful. Amazingly, we managed to visit the family of one of our classmates from college. They were extremely generous. They made us some traditional *feijoada* – a bean and meat dish. It was delicious! I could happily spend another month here. We'll have to come back and visit again.

Comments

Steve: Hey Chloe. I miss you! It's cold and wet here, and I'm working, unfortunately. Have you been able to see any capoeira?

B Pair work Read the blogs again. Are the sentences true or false? Write *T* or *F*.

1. Guatemala is exactly what Jake expected. _____
2. The weather has been bad for his entire trip. _____
3. He had problems with his tent one night. _____
4. Chloe enjoyed Carnival. _____
5. She and her friends have finished sightseeing. _____
6. She would like to spend more time in Brazil. _____

2 Listening A traveler's adventures

A 🔊 1.21 Listen to Suzanne's friends talk about her trip to New Zealand. Check (✓) the things Suzanne has done.

☐ ☐ ☐ ☐ ☐

B 🔊 1.21 Listen again. Answer the questions.

1. How does Suzanne's friend know about her trip?
2. Does Suzanne like to try new things?
3. What family does Suzanne have in New Zealand? Did she meet them on her trip?
4. What are Suzanne's photos like? Why are her friends surprised?
5. Have Suzanne's friends traveled a lot?

3 Writing and speaking Blog about it

A Read the excerpt from a blog below and the Help note. Underline the adverbs of attitude in the blog.

FLYING ABOVE THE RAIN FOREST

Last summer, I went on the Sky Trek in the rain forest in Monteverde, Costa Rica. I'm afraid of heights, so I almost didn't go. Fortunately, there were some great guides, and they really helped me. Amazingly, it wasn't really scary. It was the most exciting experience I've ever had! I didn't see a quetzal bird, unfortunately, so I'll just have to go back.

📝 Help note

Adverbs of attitude
Use adverbs like **fortunately**, **unfortunately**, **amazingly**, etc., to show your attitude or feeling about something.

> **Fortunately,** there were some great guides.
> I didn't see a quetzal bird, **unfortunately**.
> **Amazingly,** it wasn't really scary.

About you **B** Write a blog entry about an exciting experience you've had. Use *fortunately*, *unfortunately*, and *amazingly*. Do you have a photo to add to the blog?

C Class activity Take turns reading your classmates' blogs. Discuss who has . . .

- had the most exciting experience.
- done something you'd love to do.
- been somewhere you'd love to go.

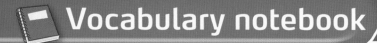

Vocabulary notebook / Have you ever . . . ?

Learning tip *Verb charts*

When you learn a new verb, write the three main forms in a chart.

base form	simple past	past participle
go	went	gone

The top 10 past participles after *I've never*. . . are:

1. been	6. done
2. heard	7. gone
3. had	8. read
4. seen	9. used
5. tried	10. watched

1 Word builder Complete the charts.

These verbs have three different forms.

be	was / were	been		drive	drove			break		broken
do	did			write		written		choose	chose	
go		gone		eat	ate			speak		spoken
see	saw			give		given		wake	woke	
drink		drunk		fall	fell			get		gotten
sing	sang			take		taken		forget	forgot	

2 Make a chart like the one above for the verbs below. Note the simple past form is the same as the past participle.

bring	catch	have	keep	make	read	sell	teach	think
buy	find	hear	leave	meet	say	sit	tell	win

3 Now complete these charts.

The base forms and past participles are the same.

become	became	become
come		
run		

All forms are the same.

cut	cut	cut
hurt		
put		

On your own

Make a "sentence string." Complete the sentence *I've never* . . . How many different ideas can you think of?

I've never flown a plane, danced in the rain,...

Can Do! Now I can . . .

☑ I can . . .   ? I need to review how to . . .

- ☐ talk about my dreams.
- ☐ describe experiences I've had or haven't had.
- ☐ keep a conversation going.
- ☐ show interest with *Have you?*, *Do you?*, etc.

- ☐ understand people talking about experiences.
- ☐ understand a conversation about travel.
- ☐ read a travel blog.
- ☐ write a blog about my travel experiences.

20

✓ Can Do! In this unit, you learn how to . . .

Lesson A
- Talk about your country or city using superlative adjectives and superlatives with nouns

Lesson B
- Ask and answer questions about your country's natural features with *How* + adjective

Lesson C
- Use short responses with *really* and *sure* to be a supportive listener
- Use superlatives for emphasis

Lesson D
- Read an article about world records
- Write a factual article about your country

1

Arenal Volcano in Costa Rica has been continuously active since 1968.

2

The Great Pyramid of Giza in Egypt dates from around 2560 BCE.

4

This roller coaster at Six Flags Great Adventure in New Jersey, U.S.A., has a 139-meter (456-foot) drop and goes at 206 kilometers (128 miles) per hour.

3

The Great Canyon of Yarlung Tsangpo in Tibet is deeper than the Grand Canyon in the United States.

Before you begin . . .

Have you ever done any of these things? Which would you really like to do?

- See an active volcano.
- Go hiking in a beautiful canyon.
- Visit an ancient city or monument.
- Ride a scary roller coaster.

Test your knowledge. Can you guess the answers to these questions?

1. Which city has the tallest office building in the world?
   a. Kuala Lumpur   b. Taipei   c. Chicago

This building is 509 meters (1,670 feet) tall.

2. Where is the longest suspension bridge?
   a. Japan   b. Denmark   c. China

This is the longest suspension bridge in the world. It's 1,990 meters (6,529 feet) long.

3. Where is the largest shopping mall?
   a. Canada   b. China   c. The United States

This mall covers about 1.97 million square meters (6.46 million square feet).

4. Where is the busiest fast-food restaurant in the world?
   a. Seoul   b. Moscow   c. Hong Kong

This restaurant serves over 40,000 people each day.

5. Which city has the biggest soccer stadium in Europe?
   a. London   b. Dublin   c. Barcelona

This stadium has the most seats. It can hold nearly 100,000 people.

6. Which country has the most tourism?
   a. The United States   b. Spain   c. France

This is the most popular country with tourists. Eighty million people visit every year.

1 Getting started

A Look at the pictures. What is the quiz about? Are you good at these kinds of quizzes?

B 🔊 1.22 Listen to the quiz. Can you guess the correct answers? Circle *a, b,* or *c*. Then compare with a partner. Check your answers on the last page of your book.

Figure it out **C** **Pair work** Complete the questions. Then ask and answer them with a partner. Can you guess the correct answers? Check your answers on the last page of your book.

1. What's the _____ (big) train station in the world?

2. What's the _____ (busy) airport in the world?

3. Where is the _____ (large) building in the world?

4. What's the _____ (expensive) city in the world?

2 Grammar Superlatives ◀)) 1.23

Extra practice p. 142

For short adjectives *the* + adjective + *-est*	What's **the tallest** building in the world? What's **the busiest** restaurant?
For long adjectives *the* + *most / least* + adjective	What's **the most interesting** city in your country? What's **the least expensive** store?
Irregular superlatives *good* ▸ *the best*; *bad* ▸ *the worst*	What's **the best** country to visit? What's **the worst** problem in your country?
Superlatives with nouns *the most* + noun	Which country has **the most tourism**? Which stadium has **the most seats**?

A Complete these questions about your country. Use the superlative form of the adjectives or the superlative with nouns.

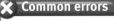

In conversation

The most + adjective is about 20 times more common than *the least* + adjective.

1. What's __the largest__ (large) city?
2. Which airport has _____ (flights) every day?
3. What's _____ (fast) way to travel?
4. What's _____ (beautiful) region?
5. Which city has _____ (tourism)?
6. Where's _____ (famous) monument?
7. What's _____ (good) university?
8. What's _____ (bad) problem for people?
9. Which city has _____ (big) population?

✕ Common errors

Use *-est* with short adjectives.

*What's the **tallest** building in your city?*
(NOT *What's the ~~most tall~~ building in your city?*)

About you **B** **Pair work** Ask and answer the questions.
Do you and your partner agree on the answers?

3 Speaking naturally Linking and deletion with superlatives

Link the final *st* to vowel sounds and the sounds / h, l, r, w, y /. *What's the mo**st i**nteresting neighborhood?* *What's the talle**st o**ffice building?* *What's the bigge**st h**otel?* *What's the large**st l**ibrary?* *What's the nice**st r**estaurant?* *What's the faste**st w**ay to travel around?* *What's the olde**st u**niversity?*	**Delete the final *t* and link the *s* to most consonant sounds.** *What area has the mo**s(t) t**raffic?* *What's the busie**s(t) m**all or shopping area?* *Where's the bigge**s(t) s**tadium?* *What's the be**s(t) s**ports team?* *What neighborhood has the mo**s(t) c**lubs?* *What's the mo**s(t) p**opular dance club?* *What's the be**s(t) m**ovie theater?*

A ◀)) 1.24 Listen and repeat the questions above. Notice how the final *st* is linked to vowel sounds and the sounds /h, l, r, w, y/. However, the final *t* is deleted before – and the *s* is linked to – most consonant sounds.

About you **B** **Pair work** Ask and answer the questions above about your city. Agree on an answer for each question. Then compare with your classmates.

1 Building vocabulary and grammar

A Complete the facts below with seven of the natural features in the box. Which facts did you know?

| archipelago | desert | island | mountain | rain forest | ✓river |
| coast | glacier | lake | ocean | reef | volcano |

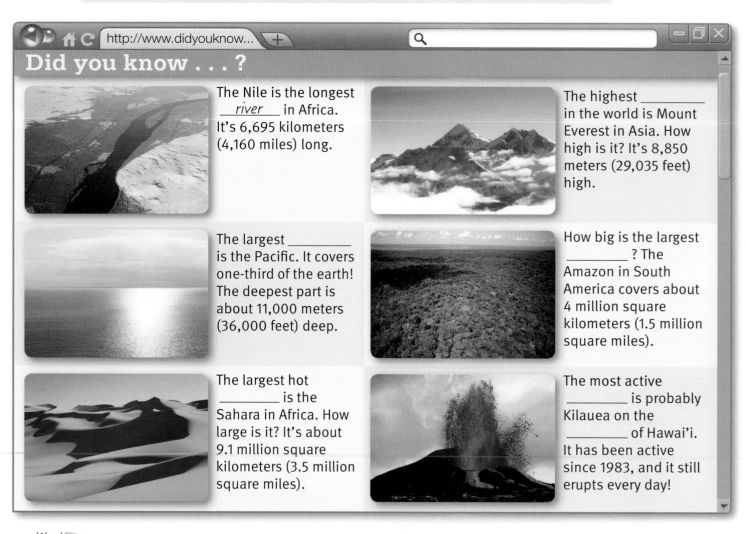

http://www.didyouknow...

Did you know . . . ?

The Nile is the longest _river_ in Africa. It's 6,695 kilometers (4,160 miles) long.

The highest _____ in the world is Mount Everest in Asia. How high is it? It's 8,850 meters (29,035 feet) high.

The largest _____ is the Pacific. It covers one-third of the earth! The deepest part is about 11,000 meters (36,000 feet) deep.

How big is the largest _____ ? The Amazon in South America covers about 4 million square kilometers (1.5 million square miles).

The largest hot _____ is the Sahara in Africa. How large is it? It's about 9.1 million square kilometers (3.5 million square miles).

The most active _____ is probably Kilauea on the _____ of Hawai'i. It has been active since 1983, and it still erupts every day!

Word sort **B** What natural features are in your country? Complete the chart. Then compare with a partner.

Features we have		Features we don't have	
beaches		desert	

Vocabulary notebook p. 30

"We have a lot of great beaches. They're some of the best in the world."

Figure it out **C** Can you complete the questions and answers?

1. How _____ is the Nile River?
2. _____ high is Mount Everest?
3. It's 6,695 kilometers _____ .
4. It's 8,850 meters _____ .

2 Grammar Questions with *How* + adjective . . . ? 🔊 1.25

Extra practice p. 142

How high is Mount Everest?   It's 8,850 meters (29,035 feet) **high**.
How long is the Nile River?   It's 6,695 kilometers (4,160 miles) **long**.
How wide is the Grand Canyon?   It's about 29 kilometers (18 miles) **wide**.
How deep is the Pacific Ocean?   It's about 11,000 meters (36,000 feet) **deep**.
How large is the Sahara Desert?   It's 9.1 million square kilometers (3.5 million square miles).
How hot does it get in Death Valley?   It can reach 48 degrees Celsius (120 degrees Fahrenheit).

Some measurements can be followed by an adjective: *high, tall, long, wide, deep*

A Write two questions about each of the natural features below.

Questions
1. the longest river in Canada
2. the highest mountain in South America
3. the smallest continent
4. the widest canyon in the world
5. the deepest lake in the world
6. the coldest place in the world

Answers
1. The Mackenzie River / 4,241 kilometers
2. Mount Aconcagua / 6,962 meters
3. Australia / almost 7.7 million square kilometers
4. The Grand Canyon / 29 kilometers
5. Lake Baikal / 1,741 meters
6. Antarctica / −89.6 degrees Celsius

What's the longest river in Canada? How long is it?

B **Pair work** Ask and answer your questions.
Use the information given above.

A What's the longest river in Canada?   *A How long is it?*
B The Mackenzie River.   *B It's 4,241 kilometers long.*

3 Listening What do you know?

A **Pair work** Take the quiz below. Circle *a*, *b*, or *c*, and guess the answers to the questions.

1. The world's tallest trees grow in _____ .
   a. Japan   c. the United States
   b. Brazil
   How tall are they? They're _____ .

2. _____ is the highest lake in the world.
   a. Lake Victoria   c. Lake Superior
   b. Lake Titicaca
   How high is it? It's _____ .

3. The longest mountain range is _____ .
   a. the Andes   c. the Rocky Mountains
   b. the Himalayas
   How long is it? It's _____ .

4. The world's largest archipelago is _____ .
   a. the Philippines   c. Indonesia
   b. Greece
   How many islands does it have? It has _____ .

5. The world's deepest canyon is in _____ .
   a. the United States   c. Australia
   b. Tibet
   How deep is it? It's _____ .

6. The world's smallest volcano is in _____ .
   a. the Philippines   c. Mexico
   b. Italy
   How high is it? It's _____ .

B 🔊 1.26 **Pair work** Listen to the quiz show. Were your guesses correct?
Write the correct answers above.

Sounds right p. 137

I had the best time.

1 Conversation strategy Being a supportive listener

A Are there any national parks in your country? Which one is the most beautiful? Which one is the largest?

B 🔊 1.27 Listen to Kim and Diego. What do they say about Sequoia National Park?

Kim	This is the most incredible place!
Diego	Yeah, it really is. It feels good to be out of the city.
Kim	It sure does. You know, these trees are just awesome.
Diego	They really are. Have you ever been to Sequoia National Park?
Kim	No. Have you?
Diego	Yeah. I went last year. The trees there are the tallest in the world.
Kim	Really? I didn't know that.
Diego	Yeah. I had the best time. I mean, it's just the greatest place to hike.
Kim	We should go hiking there sometime.
Diego	You're right. We really should.

C **Notice** how Kim and Diego use short responses sometimes with *really* and *sure* to agree and to be supportive listeners. Find examples in the conversation.

"This is the most incredible place!"
"Yeah, it really is."

D Match the comments on the left with the responses on the right. Then practice with a partner.

1. The weather was <u>great</u> last Saturday. _____
2. This city doesn't have many <u>parks</u>. _____
3. We should <u>go hiking</u> sometime. _____
4. <u>The lake</u> here is a great place to go swimming. _____
5. I like being out of the city. You can <u>hear the birds</u>. _____

a. You're right. We really should.
b. Yeah, you sure can.
c. Yeah. It sure is.
d. It really was. I spent the whole day outdoors.
e. No, it really doesn't. That's too bad.

About you **E** **Pair work** Practice the comments and responses using your own ideas. Change the underlined words.

2 Strategy plus Using superlatives for emphasis

You can use superlatives to emphasize your opinions or feelings.

This is the most incredible place!

I had the best time.

About you **Pair work** Complete the answers with the superlative form of the adjectives. Then practice with a partner. Practice again with your own information.

1. A Where's your favorite place to hang out?
    B Well, I really like going to cafés. You see _____ (interesting) people.
2. A Where's a good place to go to get out of the city?
    B I like going into the mountains. It's so quiet, and you can see _____ (amazing) wildlife.
3. A I heard that you can take a boat trip down the river.
    B You sure can. You can get _____ (good) views of the city. You really should do it.
4. A How was your vacation? Was it fun?
    B Yeah. We went sailing around some islands. I had _____ (good) time.

3 Listening and strategies Travel talk

A 🔊 **1.28** Listen to a radio interview. Number the experiences 1 to 4 in the order you hear them.

☐ A Caribbean cruise

☐ A visit to Petra, Jordan

☐ A trip to Antarctica

☐ A train ride through Copper Canyon in Mexico

B 🔊 **1.28** Listen again. How does Jill answer these questions? Complete the sentences.

1. What's the most interesting place you've ever been to? Petra. It's _____.
2. What's the most beautiful place you've seen? Antarctica has _____.
3. What's the best trip you've taken? Copper Canyon. The colors _____.
4. What's the most exciting thing you've done on a trip? I rode _____.
5. What was your worst trip? A Caribbean cruise. The cruise was great, but I _____.

About you **C** **Group work** Discuss the questions. What experiences have people in your group had?

A Well, I went to Rome one time. I had the best time. It's fun to explore new places.
B Yeah, it sure is. I bet Rome was amazing.

Free talk p. 130

1 Reading

Reading tip

Before you read, try and answer the questions. Then read to check your guesses.

A Read the questions in the article. Can you guess the correct answers? Then read the article. Were your guesses correct?

World Records

What was more popular?

☐ A family video uploaded online showing a baby biting his older brother's finger

☐ A popular video war game

"Charlie bit my finger" made the record books as the most liked video in one year with 908,668 "likes." The video war game, however, sold 6.5 million copies in the first 24 hours of its launch in the United States and UK alone.

What's the longest?

☐ The longest snake in the world   ☐ The shortest street   ☐ The world record for the long jump

The world's longest snake, a python, is 7.67 meters (25 feet 2 inches) long. It's the scariest inhabitant at a haunted house attraction in Kansas City, Missouri.

Meanwhile, the shortest street in the world, in Caithness, Scotland, is only 2 meters (6 feet 9 inches) long. It consists of one house with the address 1, Ebenezer Place.

The world record for the long jump was set in 1991. Mike Powell from the United States jumped 8.95 meters (29 feet 4.36 inches) in Tokyo, Japan. More than two decades later, it was still the world record.

Which is more dangerous?

☐ The most dangerous road in world   ☐ The most dangerous animal

The most dangerous road in the world runs 69 kilometers (43 miles) from La Paz to Coroico in Bolivia. On average there are 300 deaths annually. The road is most dangerous in the rainy season when it is muddy and wet.

The deadliest animal is the mosquito. This tiny insect can carry a deadly disease, malaria. Malaria kills more than two million people a year.

Which is older?

☐ The oldest skyscraper city   ☐ The oldest living tree

The oldest skyscraper city in the world is in Yemen. Shibam, with approximately 7,000 citizens, has buildings up to 12 stories high. While they are not the tallest skyscrapers in the world (the tallest is currently in Dubai, UAE), they are the oldest. Most of the 500 skyscrapers were built in the sixteenth century. However, Hong Kong, the place with the *most* skyscrapers, has 2,354 towering buildings, which together would almost reach a space station orbiting Earth.

Some of the oldest forests in the world are in the Andes, a mountain range in southern Chile and Argentina. The average age of these forests is 2,500 years old. However, the oldest living tree, a pine tree in the White Mountains of California, is 4,800 years old.

B Read the article again. Circle the correct words to make the sentences true according to the article.

1. The most popular video war game sold 6.5 million copies in one **day / month**.
2. The longest snake is **shorter / longer** than the world's longest long jump.
3. The people at 1, Ebenezer Place have **no / a few** next-door neighbors.
4. The worst time for accidents on the road is during the **wet / cold** season.
5. **Shibam / Dubai / Hong Kong** has the most skyscrapers.
6. The oldest living tree **is / is not** in one of the oldest forests.

C Find the bold words in the article. Then choose *a* or *b* to complete the sentences.

1. After a **launch,** a company starts to _____ a product.   a. sell   b. design
2. An **inhabitant** is a thing or person that _____ a place.   a. visits   b. lives in
3. If a street **consists of** one house, it means it _____ one house.   a. has   b. is famous for
4. When something happens **annually**, it happens every _____ .   a. month   b. year
5. A city that has 7,000 **citizens** has 7,000 _____ .   a. people   b. buildings
6. A **towering** building is very _____ .   a. short   b. tall

2 Speaking and writing Interesting facts

A **Group work** Discuss these questions about your country. Find out as many facts as you can about each thing. Take notes.

What is . . .

- the highest mountain? the longest river?
- the longest bridge? the tallest building?
- the best-known natural feature?
- the best time of year to visit?
- the city with the most historic sites?

B Read the article and the Help note. Then write an article about an interesting place in your country. Add information as shown in the Help note. Include a photo if you can.

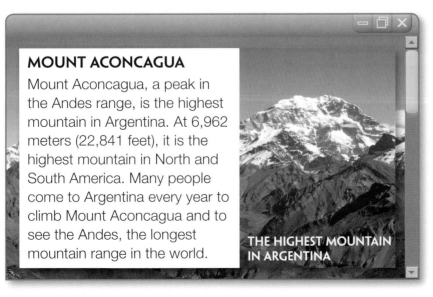

MOUNT ACONCAGUA

Mount Aconcagua, a peak in the Andes range, is the highest mountain in Argentina. At 6,962 meters (22,841 feet), it is the highest mountain in North and South America. Many people come to Argentina every year to climb Mount Aconcagua and to see the Andes, the longest mountain range in the world.

THE HIGHEST MOUNTAIN IN ARGENTINA

Help note

Adding information

Mount Aconcagua is the highest mountain in Argentina. + It is a peak in the Andes range. =

*Mount Aconcagua, **a peak in the Andes range**, is the highest mountain in Argentina.*

Many people come to Argentina to see the Andes. + They are the longest mountain range in the world. =

*Many people come to Argentina to see the Andes, **the longest mountain range in the world**.*

C **Group work** Take turns reading your articles aloud. What new information did you learn?

Learning tip *Drawing maps*

Draw a map of your country. Include natural features.
Label your map.

In conversation

The six natural features people talk
about most are:

1. lakes	3. mountains	5. oceans
2. beaches	4. rivers	6. valleys

1 Fill in the missing labels
on this map of Australia.

archipelago	mountains
bridge	ocean
coast	rain forest
desert	reef
island	river
lake	volcano

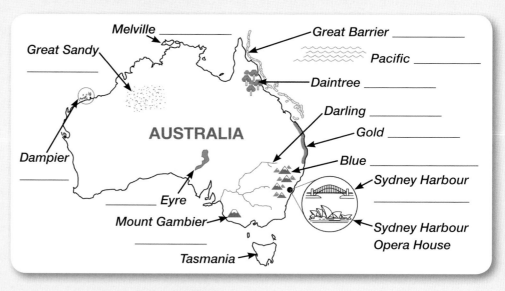

2 **Word builder** Sketch a map of your country. Draw and label
natural features. Are any of these features in your country?

bay   cliffs   geysers   hot springs   peninsula   sand dunes   waterfall

On your own

Find out the highest, longest, biggest,
deepest, and largest natural features in your
country. Make a fact chart showing how
long, high, big, and deep the features are.

Can Do! Now I can . . .

✔ I can . . .	? I need to review how to . . .

☐ talk about the best, worst, and most beautiful things in
my city and country.

☐ describe natural features.

☐ use short responses to be a supportive listener.

☐ emphasize my opinions and feelings using superlatives.

☐ understand a quiz about natural features.

☐ understand an interview about someone's
travel experiences.

☐ read an article about world records.

☐ write a factual article about my country.

1 How much do you know about your partner?

A Complete the sentences with an adverb or adjective. Then make guesses about your partner by circling the affirmative or negative form of the verb.

Your guesses My partner . . .	Are your guesses . . .	
	right?	wrong?
1. (eats)/ doesn't eat ___slowly___ (slow).	☐	☐
2. **listens / doesn't listen** _____ (careful) to the weather forecast.	☐	☐
3. **can draw / can't draw** really _____ (good).	☐	☐
4. **gets / doesn't get** upset _____ (easy).	☐	☐
5. **feels / doesn't feel** _____ (bad) if he / she can't do a job _____ (proper).	☐	☐
6. **tries / doesn't try** _____ (hard) to be on time for appointments.	☐	☐

B **Pair work** Ask and answer questions to check your guesses. Show interest in what your partner says.

A *I guessed that you eat slowly. Do you?*

B *Actually, I do. I'm always the last person to finish a meal.*

A *You are? Well, it's probably a good idea to eat slowly.*

2 Have you ever?

Pair work Find out if your partner has ever done any of these things. Ask and answer questions. Give more information in your "yes" answers.

see someone famous	eat something unusual	win a prize or a competition	be late for an important event	break a bone
get sick and miss a class	have an argument	lose something important	buy yourself something special	throw a party

A *Have you ever seen someone famous?*

B *Yes, I have. I saw Taylor Swift in concert last July.*

3 What natural and human wonders would you like to see?

Complete the chart with four natural and four human wonders. Then discuss with a partner.

Natural wonders	Human wonders
volcano - Mt. Fuji	

"I'd really like to see Mt. Fuji. I've never seen it before. Have you seen it?"

4 Can you complete this conversation?

Complete the conversation with the words and expressions in the box. Use capital letters where necessary. Then practice with a partner.

| I've ever seen | We really should | Have you | at least | incredibly |
| ✓ I've heard | We sure did | I saw | always | the coolest |

Milton Have you been to the new sports complex?

Peter No, but ___I've heard___ it's fabulous. How about you?

Milton Actually, I've been there every weekend this summer.

Peter _____? What's it like?

Milton Great. You see _____ people there. _____ Jillian and Maggie there Saturday. They're _____ hanging out at the skating rink.

Peter Maybe we should go skating there sometime.

Milton Yeah. _____ .

Peter So, what's the pool there like?

Milton Gigantic. I think it's the biggest pool _____ .

Peter Do you remember that little pool in Lincoln Park?

Milton Yeah. We always had a lot of fun there.

Peter _____ . But it was _____ small.

Milton Yeah, but _____ it was free. It costs $20 to swim in this new pool!

5 What do you think?

Complete the questions with superlatives. Then ask and answer the questions with a partner.

1. What's ___the tallest___ (tall) building in this city?
2. What's _____ (nice) park around here?
3. Where's _____ (good) place to sit and enjoy the view?
4. Where's _____ (expensive) restaurant in this city?
5. What's _____ (delicious) thing you've ever eaten?
6. What's _____ (bad) movie you've ever seen?
7. Who's _____ (busy) person you know?

6 What are they like?

A Add an appropriate adverb before each adjective below. Use a different adverb each time.

___extremely___ generous   _____ impatient   _____ reliable   _____ inconsiderate

_____ disorganized   _____ talented   _____ arrogant   _____ dishonest

B Pair work Think of a person for each quality above. Think of one thing this person is always doing. Tell a partner.

"My friend Cecilia is extremely generous. She's always helping people."

Family life

 Can Do! In this unit, you learn how to . . .

Lesson A
- Talk about family life using *let, make, help, have, get, want, ask,* and *tell*

Lesson B
- Talk about your immediate and extended family
- Describe memories of growing up with *used to* and *would*

Lesson C
- Give opinions with expressions like *If you ask me*
- Agree with opinions using expressions like *Absolutely* and *That's true*

Lesson D
- Read a blog about family meals
- Write a blog entry about a family memory

1

2

3

4

Before you begin . . .

What activities do you and your family do together?
Tell the class three things.

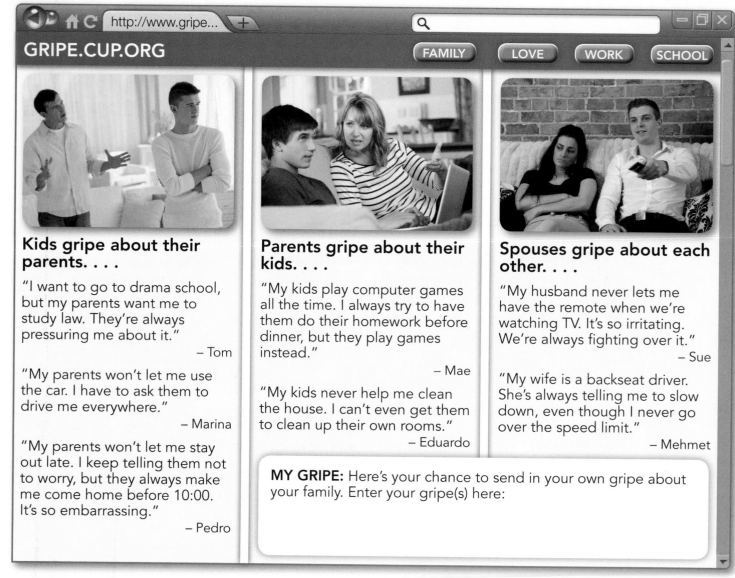

GRIPE.CUP.ORG

FAMILY   LOVE   WORK   SCHOOL

Kids gripe about their parents. . . .

"I want to go to drama school, but my parents want me to study law. They're always pressuring me about it."

– Tom

"My parents won't let me use the car. I have to ask them to drive me everywhere."

– Marina

"My parents won't let me stay out late. I keep telling them not to worry, but they always make me come home before 10:00. It's so embarrassing."

– Pedro

Parents gripe about their kids. . . .

"My kids play computer games all the time. I always try to have them do their homework before dinner, but they play games instead."

– Mae

"My kids never help me clean the house. I can't even get them to clean up their own rooms."

– Eduardo

Spouses gripe about each other. . . .

"My husband never lets me have the remote when we're watching TV. It's so irritating. We're always fighting over it."

– Sue

"My wife is a backseat driver. She's always telling me to slow down, even though I never go over the speed limit."

– Mehmet

MY GRIPE: Here's your chance to send in your own gripe about your family. Enter your gripe(s) here:

1 Getting started

A **What are some things family members argue about? Add your own ideas. Tell the class.**

| chores   school   sharing things   staying out late |

B 🔊 **2.01 Listen and read the messages on the website above. What problems do the people have?**

Figure it out **C** **Complete sentences about the people above. Add verbs.**

1. Marina's parents won't let her _____ the car.
2. Pedro's parents make him _____ home before 10:00.
3. Mae tries to have her kids _____ their homework before dinner.
4. Eduardo can't get his kids _____ their rooms.
5. Mehmet's wife always tells him _____ even when he's not driving fast.

About you **D** **Pair work** Do you have the same gripes as the ones on the website? Tell a partner.

34

2 Grammar *let, make, help, have, get, want, ask, tell* 🔊 2.02

Extra practice p. 143

let / make / help / have + object + verb	*get / want / ask / tell* + object + *to* + verb
My parents won't **let me stay out** late.	I can't **get them to clean up** their rooms.
They **make me come** home before 10:00.	My parents **want me to study** law.
My kids never **help me clean** the house.	I have to **ask them to drive** me everywhere.
I **have them do** their homework before dinner.	My wife is always **telling me to slow down**.

A Choose the correct verbs to complete the sentences.

In conversation

You can also say *help me to do something*, but this is much less common.

███████████████ *help* + verb
██ *help* + *to* + verb

1. When I was a kid, my parents never ___*let*___ me walk to school by myself. (got / let)

2. My parents made me _____ to bed at 8:00. (go / to go)

3. My mother couldn't _____ me to eat fish. I was a picky eater! (make / get)

✖ Common errors

Don't use *to* with *let, make,* or *have*.

They make me **come** *home before 10:00.* (NOT *They make me ~~to~~ come home . . .*)

4. My brother never lets me _____ his computer. (use / to use)

5. My parents _____ me to spend more time with them. I should, but I'm too busy. (want / have)

6. My dad's always telling me _____ more exercise. (get / to get)

7. I always _____ my husband make breakfast on weekends so I can sleep late. (have / get)

8. I think kids should _____ their parents clean the house. (get / help)

9. My parents always say they want me _____ happy, not rich. (to be / be)

10. I usually _____ my parents know when I'm going to be home late. (let / have)

About you B Pair work Make five of the sentences above true for you. Tell a partner.

A *When I was a kid, my parents never let me eat junk food.*
B *Really? My parents let me have soda and stuff, but they made me eat vegetables, too.*

3 Listening and speaking Reasonable demands?

A Read the list of demands that parents make on their children. What other demands do parents make?

My parents want me to . . .

1. _____ get married and start a family.
2. _____ study a subject I'm not interested in.
3. _____ work in the family business.
4. _____ change my appearance.
5. _____ call them every week.
6. _____ move nearer to them.

B 🔊 2.03 Listen to five people talk about their parents' demands. Number the demands they talk about above 1 to 5. There is one extra.

About you C Pair work What demands do your parents or your friends' parents make? Why? Which demands are reasonable? Which are not? Tell a partner.

"My parents don't want me to get married too soon. They want me to finish college first."

1 Building vocabulary and grammar

A ◀)) **2.04** Listen and read the article. What memories do these people have?

Happiest Memories

We asked people to send us a photo and write about their happiest childhood memory.

My happiest memory is of my **great-grandmother**. She always used to keep candy in her pockets, and she'd always give us some when we came to visit. My dad used to tease us and say, "Grandma, don't give them any candy!" But she did anyway.

— Rosa, Guadalajara, Mexico

All my **aunts** and **uncles** used to come over for Sunday dinner, and there were always about 12 of us around a gigantic table. My **cousins** and I would crawl under it during dinner and play. I'm **an only child**, so it was nice to be part of a big **extended family**.

— Vasily, Saint Petersburg, Russia

My sister and **brother-in-law** used to live next door. I'm only a little older than my sister's kids, so I kind of grew up with my **niece** and **nephew**. I used to go over there a lot, and we'd play together. I was their favorite **aunt**!

— Haruka, Sendai, Japan

I used to love playing basketball with my four brothers. I grew up in a **blended family**, with two **stepbrothers** and two **half brothers**. After my parents **got divorced**, my father **married** a woman with two sons, and they had two more kids together. Anyway, the five of us used to play on a team, and we would always win.

— Justin, Vancouver, Canada

Word sort **B** Complete the chart with male or female family members and with other expressions. Add more ideas. Then tell a partner about your family.

Immediate family		Blended family		Extended family		
father	*mother*	stepfather				great-grandmother
	sister		stepsister	grandfather		
husband		stepson				aunt
	daughter		half sister	(first / second) cousin		
Other expressions					niece	
only child		*fiancé*		brother-in-law		

"I'm an only child, but I have six first cousins."

Vocabulary notebook p. 42

Figure it out **C** Underline all the examples of *used to* and *would / 'd* in the article. Are these activities and situations in the past or present? Are they finished, or do they still continue?

2 Grammar *used to* and *would* ◀)) 2.05

Extra practice p. 143

Use *used to* for regular activities or situations in the past that don't happen now or are no longer true.

I **used to go** over to my sister's house a lot.
My grandmother **used to keep** candy in her pockets.
The five of us **used to play** on a team.

Negatives and questions with *use to* are less common.

I **didn't use to like** jazz.
What kind of music **did** you **use to like**?

Use *would* or *'d* for regular activities in the past.

▶ I**'d play** with my niece and nephew.
▶ She**'d** always **give** us some.
▶ We **would** always **win**.

Don't use *would* for situations in the past.

My sister **used to live** next door.
(NOT My sister ~~would live~~ next door.)

> 💬 **In conversation**
> People often begin a story with *used to* and then continue with *would*.

About you What family memories do you have? Complete each sentence and add a sentence with *would*. Then compare your memories with a partner.

1. My family used to go to <u>*the beach*</u> in the summer. *We'd go almost every weekend.*
2. My mother used to make _____ for us.
3. My brother / sister and I used to play _____ together.
4. My family used to watch _____ on TV.
5. I used to see my aunts, uncles, and cousins _____ .
6. My grandparents used to take me to _____ .
7. My family always used to _____ on Sundays.
8. My parents didn't use to _____ on weekends.

> ✗ **Common errors**
> Don't use *used to* to talk about your routines in the present.
>
> I **used to** *skip lunch, but now I usually have a sandwich.*
> (NOT . . . ~~now I used to~~ *have a sandwich.*)

A **My family used to go to the beach in the summer. We'd go almost every weekend.**

B **Really? I bet that was fun. My family used to visit my grandmother . . .**

3 Speaking naturally *used to*

We **used to** *visit my great-grandmother.*   I **used to** *play with my cousins.*

A ◀)) 2.06 **Listen and repeat the sentences above. Notice the reduction of *used to*.**

B ◀)) 2.07 **Now listen and repeat these sentences.**

1. I used to love jumping rope.
2. I used to hate spinach.
3. I used to be afraid of spiders.
4. We used to have a cat.
5. My sister used to tease me a lot.

About you C **Pair work** Use the ideas above to talk about your childhood.

A *When I was a child, I used to love playing hopscotch.*

B *Me too. And I also used to like . . .*

(((• **Sounds right** p. 137

1 Conversation strategy Giving opinions

A Check the statements you agree with. Tell the class.

☐ People spend too much time at work.   ☐ Life is much simpler now than it used to be.

☐ Everybody's getting burned out.   ☐ People don't have enough time to relax.

B 🔊 2.08 Listen. Which of the statements above do Corey and Rob agree with?

Rob	So, how are you and Charles doing? And the kids?
Corey	Good, thanks. Just way too busy. I don't think we get enough time together. I guess it's the same for everybody.
Rob	Oh, definitely. If you ask me, we all work too much these days.
Corey	Absolutely. With all the long hours and running the kids around . . .
Rob	Oh, I know. And my wife often brings work home on the weekends, too. Whatever happened to time off?
Corey	Yeah. It seems like we don't get enough time to relax.
Rob	Oh, that's for sure. And it seems to me that's why people often get burned out.
Corey	Exactly.

C **Notice** how Rob and Corey use expressions like these to give opinions. Find examples in the conversation.

I think . . .   *It seems like . . .*

I don't think . . .   *If you ask me, . . .*

It seems to me (that) . . .

About you **D** Complete these sentences with expressions from above to give your opinions. Then compare with a partner.

1. _____ people work longer hours than they used to.

2. _____ people don't spend enough time with their families.

3. _____ it's not a good idea to take work home on the weekends.

4. _____ people should get more time off.

5. _____ there's a lot of pressure to work long hours.

6. _____ everyone is way too busy these days.

A It seems to me that people don't spend enough time with their families.

B Oh, I know. A lot of parents work long hours and have no time for their kids.

38

2 Strategy plus Agreeing

You can use these expressions to agree with people's opinions.

Absolutely.	You're right.	I agree (with you).
Definitely.	That's true.	(Oh,) yeah.
Exactly.	That's for sure.	(Oh,) I know.

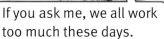

If you ask me, we all work too much these days.

Absolutely.

In conversation

Exactly, definitely, and *absolutely* are in the top 600 words.

A 🔊 2.09 **Listen to the start of five conversations. Number the responses 1 to 5.**

a. _____ Definitely. My kids love to spend time with my mother. They say she's more fun than me.

b. _____ Exactly. Some kids never want to sit down and eat with their families.

c. _____ Oh, I agree. I mean, a lot of kids stay up all night studying for exams.

d. _____ Oh, I know. But working a few hours a week can be a good experience for teenagers.

e. _____ That's true. But a lot of families need two incomes these days.

B 🔊 2.10 **Now listen and check. Do you agree with the opinions? Tell your partner.**

3 Strategies In my opinion

A Choose the best responses to complete the conversations. Then practice.

a. I've heard that one in three marriages ends in divorce. I think it's terrible for the kids.
b. If you ask me, it's better to have lots of different friends at that age.
c. I mean, it takes a long time to plan a wedding.
d. It seems to me that it's better to wait until you're a little older.

1. A It seems like people are getting married much later these days.

   B Yeah, that's true. _____

   A Definitely. That way you have time to grow up and find a rewarding job.

2. A I don't think it's good for high school kids to have a serious boyfriend or girlfriend.

   B I agree. _____

   A Exactly. But it seems like teens want to grow up faster nowadays.

3. A It seems to me that long engagements are a good idea.

   B You're right. _____

   A Absolutely. And couples need time to decide where to live and everything.

4. A I think it's sad that so many people get divorced these days.

   B Oh, I know. _____

   A That's for sure. A lot of kids have a hard time when parents get divorced.

About you **B Group work Give your opinions about the topics below. Which do you agree on?**

- divorce and children
- spending time with family
- studying all night for tests
- taking work home
- teens having jobs
- the best age to get married

1 Reading

About you **A** When you were a child, did you and your family use to eat together every day? What were family meals like? Tell the class.

B Read Barbara's blog. Why does Barbara think families should eat together more often?

> **Reading tip**
> Sometimes writers state similar ideas in the first and last paragraph. This helps tie the reading together.

http://www.barbarasblog... ＋   🔍

Barbara's Blog

It seems to me that families used to eat more meals together. And nowadays, there's often a TV nearby, or someone's talking on a cell phone or texting during dinner.

My family always used to eat dinner together, no matter what. We'd wait for everyone to get home, and then we'd all sit down together. My parents never let us take food into another room to watch TV, and if the phone rang, my mom would have us tell the caller to call back later. During dinnertime conversation, everyone had a chance to talk. Back then, I was a bit quieter than my siblings, so my dad would often ask me to talk about my day. That's how we learned to share and take turns, so everyone got to join in.

Speaking of taking turns, all of us kids used to take part in either preparing the meal or cleaning up. Sometimes my mom would let me help her in the kitchen – I'd wash and chop vegetables, or things like that. We'd always have fresh food, or at least leftovers from the night before . . . no fast food or take out.

Now, I won't pretend our mealtimes were absolutely perfect. There was plenty of sibling rivalry, especially between my little brother and me. We used to fight all the time and sometimes kick each other under the table. Then our parents would intervene, telling us to "get along or else!" Nobody knew exactly what "or else" meant, but we didn't want to risk finding out.

These days, it seems like families have little time together, especially at mealtimes. I was reading an article that said children who have regular meals with their families feel less stressed, have a healthier weight, get better grades, and are less likely to get into trouble than children from families that don't eat together. I wonder if those families know what they're missing.

C Find the expressions on the left in the blog. Match each one with a similar expression.

1. no matter what _f_
2. leftovers _____
3. pretend _____
4. sibling rivalry _____
5. intervene _____
6. or else _____

    a. food remaining after a meal
    b. competition between brothers or sisters
    c. become involved in a difficult situation
    d. act like something is true that is not
    e. or something bad will happen (used as a threat)
    f. in any situation

D Read the blog again. Are these sentences true or false? For each statement below, check (✓) *T* or *F*. Correct the false statements. Then compare with a partner.

	T	F
1. Barbara's mother used to let her watch TV while she ate dinner.	☐	☐
2. As a child, Barbara was less talkative than others in the family.	☐	☐
3. The kids in Barbara's family helped make dinner and clean up.	☐	☐
4. Barbara got along well with all her siblings at dinnertime.	☐	☐
5. Barbara thinks kids are healthier when they eat with their families.	☐	☐

2 Listening and writing Family memories

A 🔊 **2.11** Listen to three people talk about their memories of family life. What did they use to do? Number the pictures.

B 🔊 **2.11** Listen again. Why don't the people do these things now? Write a reason for each one on the line. Compare with a partner.

About you **C** **Pair work** Think of three things you used to do with your family. Tell a partner.

A We used to go skiing every winter, but my dad hurt his knee, so we stopped.

B Really? My parents didn't let us go skiing because they thought it was too dangerous.

D Read the blog below and the Help note. Underline the time markers. Then write a blog about a family memory from your childhood.

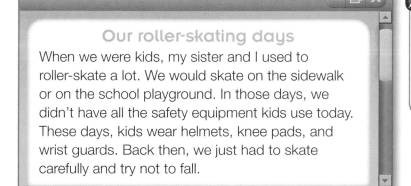

Our roller-skating days

When we were kids, my sister and I used to roller-skate a lot. We would skate on the sidewalk or on the school playground. In those days, we didn't have all the safety equipment kids use today. These days, kids wear helmets, knee pads, and wrist guards. Back then, we just had to skate carefully and try not to fall.

Help note

Using time markers
- Use these time markers to show the past:
  When we were kids, . . . / When I was . . . , In those days, . . . / Back then, . . .
- Use these time markers to show the present:
  today, now, nowadays, these days

E **Group work** Read your classmates' blogs. Then ask questions to find out more information.

"Did you use to skate to school?" *"Did your parents let you play outside by yourself?"*

Free talk p. 131

Learning tip *Word webs*

Use word webs to log new vocabulary about your family members.
What memories do you associate with each person?

1   Look at the picture. Complete the word web with memories of the grandfather in the picture.

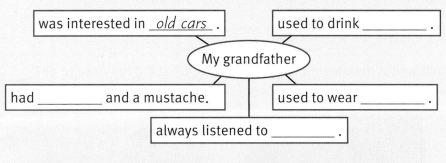

| was interested in *old cars* . | used to drink _____ . |

My grandfather

| had _____ and a mustache. | used to wear _____ . |

always listened to _____ .

2   Make word webs like the one above about two people in
your family. How many memories can you think of?

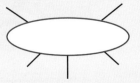 

3   **Word builder** Do you know this vocabulary? Find out the meanings of any words you don't know.
Try to add some of the words to your word webs.

adopted   ex-husband   great-aunt   separated   single parent

On your own

Make a photo album of your family. Find
photos of each of your relatives. Write their
names and a short memory about each picture.

Aunt Emily used to bake me cookies.

Can Do!   Now I can . . .

✓ I can . . .   ? I need to review how to . . .

- ☐ talk about my family life and habits.
- ☐ share my memories of growing up.
- ☐ describe things that happened in the past that don't happen now.
- ☐ give my opinions.
- ☐ use expressions like *Absolutely*, *Definitely*, etc.

- ☐ understand people talking about demands their parents make on them.
- ☐ understand people discussing things they used to do.
- ☐ read a blog about family meals.
- ☐ write a blog entry about a family memory.

Can Do! In this unit, you learn how to . . .

Lesson A
- Talk about eating habits using expressions like *a bottle of, a little, a few, very little,* and *very few*

Lesson B
- Talk about different ways to cook food
- Talk about food using *too, too much, too many,* and *enough*

Lesson C
- Respond to suggestions by letting the other person decide
- Refuse offers politely with expressions like *No, thanks. I'm fine.*

Lesson D
- Read about snacks around the world
- Write about a dish from your country

Before you begin . . .

Can you find these things in the picture? What other food items can you find?
Have you bought any of these things recently?

- a bag of potato chips
- a bottle of ketchup
- a package of cookies
- some cartons of juice
- a box of cereal
- a loaf of bread
- a jar of mustard
- a can of soup
- a tub of margarine

What do you have in your refrigerator?

We visited three people to see what they keep in the fridge.

"Let's see, um, a carton of eggs, some milk, a pound of hamburger meat, a few slices of cheese, a jar of mustard, and a little butter. Um, there aren't many vegetables. There are just a few green peppers going bad in the vegetable drawer. I guess I should eat more vegetables."

– David Freeman

"Oh, there's lots of stuff. There's fruit – oranges, mangoes, a pineapple. And I always have plenty of fresh vegetables – broccoli, tomatoes, and carrots. And there's a carton of orange juice and a tub of margarine. I usually buy 1 percent milk because it has fewer calories. And then in the freezer there are one or two frozen dinners, but not many. We eat very few frozen meals."

– Marta Delgado

"Well, there's very little food in there because I eat out most nights. So there's just a loaf of bread, a bottle of soy sauce, a few cans of soda, and a jar of hot peppers. Yeah, there's not much food in the house."

– Chris Kim

1 Getting started

A How often does your family buy food? Do you buy groceries online? at a supermarket?

B ◀)) 2.12 Listen to the people above. Who has the healthiest food in their refrigerator?

Figure it out **C** Each person above forgot to mention two things in their refrigerator. Circle the correct words in the sentences below.

1. Chris also has **a little** / **a few** butter and a **bottle** / **carton of** orange juice.
2. Marta also has **a few** / **not much** apples and a **loaf** / **jar** of bread.
3. David also has **a bottle of** / **bottle of** ketchup and some soda. He doesn't have **much** / **many** food.

2 Grammar Talking about quantities of food ◀)) 2.13

Extra practice p. 144

Uncountable nouns

We have **a little** butter in the fridge. = *some*
There's **very little** food. = *not a lot*
I'm trying to eat **less** fat.
There's **not much** food in the house.

Countable nouns

We have **a few** slices of cheese. = *some*
We eat **very few** frozen meals. = *not a lot*
1 percent milk has **fewer** calories.
There aren't **many** vegetables.

Food containers / items

a carton of juice ▶ two cartons of juice
a loaf of bread ▶ two loaves of bread

Weights and measures

a liter of / a quart of   *1 liter = 1.1 quarts*
a kilo of / a pound of   *1 kilo = 2.2 pounds*
kilo = kilogram

✗ Common errors

Don't use *a little*, *much* or *many* + *of* + noun.

There isn't **much cheese**.
(NOT There isn't ~~much of cheese~~.)

A Choose the correct words to complete the sentences.
Then compare with a partner.

1. In my refrigerator, there's always **a jar / a jar of** spaghetti sauce and **a quart of / a few** milk.

2. In my kitchen cabinet, there's **package of / a package of** rice and **a little / a bag of** chips.

3. I try to eat healthily, so I eat **a few / not much** vegetables and **a little / very little** fruit every day.

4. I've bought **very few / very little** meat and **very few / very little** cookies recently.

5. I should eat **less / fewer** junk food. I know it doesn't have **much / many** vitamins.

6. I eat **less / little** fast food than I used to, though I still enjoy **a little / a few** fries when I can!

7. Yesterday, I had **a little / a few** chocolate as a treat.

8. We always keep a few basics in the house: a couple of **loaves of / loaf of** bread, some
cartons of / carton of milk, **a few slices of / a few** cheese, and **a few / a little** eggs.

About you **B** **Pair work** Make the sentences true for you. Compare ideas.

A In my refrigerator, there's always a jar of mayonnaise, but there's not much else!
B Yeah? We don't eat much mayonnaise, but we have a few jars of salsa.

3 Talk about it Is it good for you?

Group work Discuss these beliefs about food. Do you agree? What other beliefs are there?

It's good to eat a few nuts every day. They're very healthy.

A little chocolate can be good for you. It can improve your mood.

If you eat fewer carbohydrates and a little more fat and protein, you will lose weight more quickly.

Eating less food can help you live longer.

You should try to eat nine servings of fresh fruits and vegetables every day.

A cup of green tea every day is good for your general health.

A Do you believe it's good to eat a few nuts every day?
B Well, I don't eat many nuts, actually. They have a lot of fat in them.

Building vocabulary

A Have you eaten any of these things recently? Which do you like best?

1. (stir-)fried noodles
2. grilled shrimp
3. steamed vegetables
4. boiled eggs
5. baked potatoes
6. pickled cabbage
7. roast lamb
8. barbecued beef
9. raw fish
10. smoked fish

Word sort **B** How do you like to eat different kinds of food? Make word webs like these using the words above. Then compare with a partner.

eggs

fried

potatoes

grilled

steamed

> ***i*** **Note**
>
> **Adjectives** *fried, grilled, . . .*
> **Verbs** *fry, grill, . . .*

Vocabulary notebook p. 52

2 Speaking naturally Stressing new information

A *Do you like fried **rice**?*   B *Yes, I **love** fried rice.*   **or**   B *Actually, I prefer **steamed** rice.*

A *Do you like raw **fish**?*   B *Yes, I **love** raw fish.*   **or**   B *I've never **tried** raw fish.*

A *Have you ever eaten raw **eggs**?*   B *Yes, I eat raw eggs for **break**fast.*   **or**   B *No, I only eat **cooked** eggs.*

A ◀)) 2.14 Listen and repeat the sentences above. Notice how the stress and intonation move to the new information in the answers. Then ask and answer the questions with a partner.

About you **B** **Pair work** Ask questions like the ones above. Give your own answers.

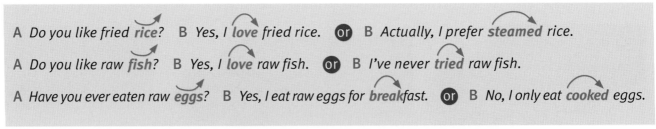

A *Do you like fried eggs?*
B *Actually, I prefer boiled eggs.*   **OR**   *No, I hate fried eggs.*

3 Building language

A 🔊 **2.15 Listen. What do Carla and Leo want to order? Practice the conversation.**

Carla Are you going to have dessert?

Leo No, I'm too full. I ate too many fries.

Carla Do you mind if I have something? My salad wasn't filling enough. I mean, is there enough time? I know I eat too slowly – probably because I talk too much!

Leo That's not true! Anyway, I want another iced tea. I'm really thirsty. I guess I put too much salt on my fries.

Carla OK. So I'm going to order some apple pie.

Leo Mmm. Sounds good. Maybe I'll have some, too.

Carla Well, as they say, there's always room for dessert!

Figure it out **B Can you complete these sentences with *enough*, *too*, *too much*, or *too many*?**

1. Leo ate _____ fries, and he put _____ salt on them.

2. Carla's still hungry because she didn't eat _____ food.

3. Leo is _____ full, but Carla isn't. Her salad wasn't filling _____ .

4. Carla eats _____ slowly. She doesn't eat fast _____ . She talks _____ .

4 Grammar *too, too much, too many,* and *enough* 🔊 2.16

Extra practice p. 144

	too / too much / too many	***enough***
With nouns	I ate **too much food / too many fries**.	I didn't eat **enough food / fries**.
As pronouns	I ate **too much / too many**.	I didn't eat **enough**.
With adjectives	He's **too full**.	Her salad wasn't **filling enough**.
With adverbs	She eats **too slowly**.	She doesn't eat **fast enough**.
With verbs	She **talks too much**.	Maybe she **doesn't listen enough**.

A Complete these sentences with *too, too much, too many,* or *enough*. More than one answer may be possible.

1. I eat _____ fast food and not _____ fruits and vegetables.

2. There's never _____ time to shop or cook during the week, so I eat out a lot.

3. During my exams, I study _____ and I don't sleep _____ .

4. I don't like fried foods – there's _____ fat in them. It's better to grill or steam food.

5. If I don't eat _____ for breakfast, or if breakfast isn't filling _____ , I'm usually _____ hungry to wait for lunch.

6. Sometimes, I eat _____ fast and I get a stomachache. Or I eat _____ .

7. I don't like ice cream. I find most desserts are _____ sweet for me.

8. I'm probably _____ careful about what I eat, but I get sick if I eat _____ fatty things.

About you **B Pair work Are the sentences above true for you? Discuss with a partner.**

A *Actually, I don't eat too much fast food. I don't eat too many fries or anything.*

B *That's good. I eat too much fast food. I don't eat properly.*

(((· Sounds right p. 138

1 Conversation strategy Letting another person decide

A What drinks or snacks do you offer visitors to your home?

B 🔊 2.17 Listen. What snack does Laura offer Kayla? What drinks does she offer?

Laura	Can I get you something to eat?
Kayla	Oh, I'm OK for now. But thanks.
Laura	Are you sure? I have some cheese in the fridge and a box of crackers.
Kayla	No, thanks. I'm fine. Really. Maybe later.
Laura	Well, how about some tea or coffee?
Kayla	Um . . . are you having some?
Laura	Yeah. I need to wake up a bit. So tea or coffee?
Kayla	Either one is fine. Whatever you're having.
Laura	OK. I think I'll make some tea. Do you want it with milk or lemon?
Kayla	Oh. Either way. Whichever is easier. Are you sure it's not too much trouble?
Laura	No, no. It's no trouble at all.

C Notice how Kayla uses expressions like these because she wants Laura to decide. Find examples in the conversation.

Either one (is fine).   *Whatever you're having.*
Either way (is fine).   *Whichever is easier (for you).*
                         Whatever you prefer.

D Pair work Write responses to these questions, letting the other person decide. Then start a conversation with a partner, and plan an evening out using the ideas below.

1. So what do you feel like doing this evening? Do you want to eat out or go to a movie?
2. OK. Let's go to a movie. What do you want to see? A thriller or a comedy or . . . ?
3. I guess we could eat out first. Do you want to eat Italian or Chinese or . . . ?
4. So, do you want to walk, or should we catch the bus? The buses run every 20 minutes.
5. Should we buy the tickets there, or should we get them online before we go?
6. Do you want a drink first? Would you like some lemonade or some iced tea?

     A *So what do you feel like doing this evening? Do you want to eat out or go to a movie?*
     B *Um, well, whatever you prefer.*

2 **Strategy plus** Polite refusals

**You can use expressions like these
to refuse offers of food and drink politely.**

No, thanks. Maybe later.
No, thanks. I'm fine. Really.
I'm OK for now. But thanks.

Can I get you something to eat?   I'm OK for now. But thanks.

**Imagine you are the guest at a party. How can you refuse your host's offers politely?
Complete the conversation. Then practice with a partner.**

Host   Would you like something to eat?

Guest   _____

Host   Really? Are you sure? There are a few sandwiches or some vegetables and dip.

Guest   _____

Host   Well, can I get you something to drink? I have juice, soda, . . . or would you prefer some water?

Guest   _____

Host   Well, if you change your mind, just let me know.

3 **Listening and strategies** That sounds good.

A 🔊 **2.18 Listen to four conversations about food and drink. Number the pictures 1 to 4.**

☐   ☐   ☐   ☐

B 🔊 **2.18 Listen again. Choose an appropriate response to the last thing you hear. Write the number
of the conversation, 1 to 4.**

a. Actually, they all look really good. Whatever you prefer. _____

b. Either one is fine. Whatever you're having. _____

c. I could go either way. You choose. _____

d. Oh, no, thanks. I'm fine. Maybe later. _____

C Choose one of the pictures and role-play a conversation.

 A So would you like some dessert? How about chocolate cake or a little ice cream or . . . ?

 B No, thanks. Maybe later. I'm too full.

Free talk p. 131

1 Reading

A Brainstorm! How many different snacks can you think of? Which ones are popular in your country? Make a class list.

B Read the article. Which snacks have you heard of? Have you tried any of them?

 Reading tip

Writers sometimes start a sentence with a short description of something before they name it. ***Originally from Spain**, empanadas are baked or deep-fried pastries. . . .*

 http://www.snacksaroundtheworld...   🔍

SNACKS AROUND THE WORLD

BAOS

Baos are delicious steamed or baked buns with a variety of fillings such as spicy meat, sweet bean, pickles, or custard. A favorite in many Asian countries, they are delicious at any meal – even breakfast. Although they have been popular for over 2,000 years, people are still coming up with new ideas for fillings – like scrambled eggs or coconut!

MOCHI ICE CREAM

In the 1980s, a Japanese company showed the world a great new way to eat ice cream. They wrapped little ice cream balls in colorful sheets of sticky rice called *mochi*. You can hold these little treats in your hand as you eat them, and the ice cream won't melt on your fingers! Now popular in many countries, frozen mochi ice cream comes in flavors like green tea, chocolate, and mango.

DOLMA

Popular throughout Mediterranean countries, *dolma* are particularly popular as a snack food in Turkey. The best-known dolma are grape leaves stuffed with tasty ground-meat fillings or rice with herbs and spices and a few nuts. (In Turkish, *dolmak* means "stuffed.") Freshly steamed, dolma are delicious with yogurt.

FLAVORED POPCORN

People never get tired of popcorn. Native Americans first ate popcorn over 2,000 years ago, and people around the world still love it today! Buy it ready-made or cook it in a little oil until it "pops." Or make your own microwaved popcorn, and add your own flavors. How about a little cheese, chocolate, or caramel on yours? Some even more creative flavors are baked potato, curry, and taco. What new popcorn flavor can you think of?

EMPANADAS

If you're in Latin America, and you're looking for a quick snack, chances are you're not far from an *empanada* stand. Originally from Spain, empanadas are baked or deep-fried pastries that have a variety of different fillings depending on the region. Traditional fillings often have meat and potatoes or meat with spices, chopped onion, egg, olives, and raisins. In southern Europe, they often have a fish filling. They make a great snack at any time of the day.

C Read the article again. Complete the chart for each snack.

Name of snack	Popular where?	Cooked? How?	Ingredients / flavors
baos	Asia	steamed / baked	spicy meat, sweet bean, . . .

2 Listening and speaking Snack habits

A Have you tried any of the snacks below? Which countries do you think they come from originally?

 hummus
 nachos
 edamame
 chocolate chip cookies

B ◄)) 2.19 Listen. How would the three people answer the questions? Complete the chart.

	Zoe	Josh	Kate
1. What's your favorite snack?			
2. When do you eat it?			
3. Do you think it's healthy?			
4. Do you know how to make it?			

About you **C** **Group work** Discuss the questions above. Complete a chart like the one above with your classmates' information. Which snacks are healthy? Which do you like?

3 Writing You should definitely try it!

A Read the Help note and the article below. What do *like*, *for example*, and *such as* give examples of?

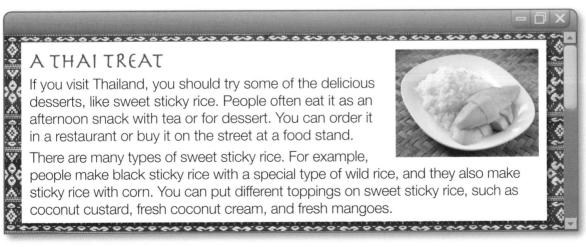

A THAI TREAT

If you visit Thailand, you should try some of the delicious desserts, like sweet sticky rice. People often eat it as an afternoon snack with tea or for dessert. You can order it in a restaurant or buy it on the street at a food stand.

There are many types of sweet sticky rice. For example, people make black sticky rice with a special type of wild rice, and they also make sticky rice with corn. You can put different toppings on sweet sticky rice, such as coconut custard, fresh coconut cream, and fresh mangoes.

Help note

Giving examples
You can introduce examples with:
like
for example
such as

B Choose a popular snack food or traditional dish in your country. Write an article about it for a food website. Include a photo if you can.

C **Class activity** Read your classmates' articles. Choose three to add to your website.

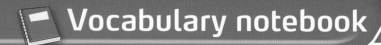

Vocabulary notebook / Fried bananas

Learning tip *Collocations – words that go together*

Learn new words in combination with other words. For example, learn adjectives that often go before a noun.

> *boiled eggs, fried eggs, raw eggs*

In conversation

The most common collocations in conversation with these six cooking words are:

1. *fried* chicken	4. *grilled* cheese
2. *boiled* eggs	5. *smoked* salmon
3. *baked* potatoes	6. *raw* fish

1 Cross out the adjective that doesn't go well with each noun.

a. fried
pickled
~~smoked~~
raw
⎤ onions

b. barbecued
steamed
fried
boiled
⎤ rice

c. stir-fried
spicy
boiled
pickled
⎤ noodles

d. smoked
fresh
canned
dried
⎤ fruit

2 How many cooking or taste words can you put before these foods? List them from your least favorite to your favorite ways of eating them in a chart like the one below.

carrots   chicken   eggs   fish   pineapple   red peppers

least favorite - - - - - - - - - - - - → favorite				
boiled	*steamed*	*stir-fried*	*raw*	carrots

3 **Word builder** Which adjective goes best with each noun? Complete the expressions.

✓creamed   dark   grated   mashed   scrambled   sweet and sour   whole   whole wheat

_____ eggs	_____ shrimp	_____ chocolate	_____ bread
_____ milk	*creamed* spinach	_____ potatoes	_____ cheese

On your own

Find a restaurant menu online and translate five of the dishes into English.

Fried bananas

Can DO! Now I can . . .

✓ I can . . .   ❓ I need to review how to . . .

- ☐ talk about quantities of food and eating habits.
- ☐ discuss different ways to cook food.
- ☐ respond to suggestions by letting the other person decide.
- ☐ use expressions like *I'm fine* to refuse offers.

- ☐ understand people offering and accepting or refusing food.
- ☐ understand conversations about snacks.
- ☐ read about snacks around the world.
- ☐ write about a dish from my country.

Managing life

UNIT 6

✓ **Can Do!** In this unit, you learn how to . . .

Lesson A
- Talk about future plans and schedules using *will*, *be going to*, the present continuous, and the simple present

Lesson B
- Discuss problems and solutions using *ought to*, *have got to*, *would rather*, *had better*, etc.
- Use expressions with *make* and *do*

Lesson C
- Use expressions like *I'd better go* to end phone conversations
- Use expressions like *Catch you later* to say good-bye

Lesson D
- Read a blog about multitasking
- Write some advice about time management

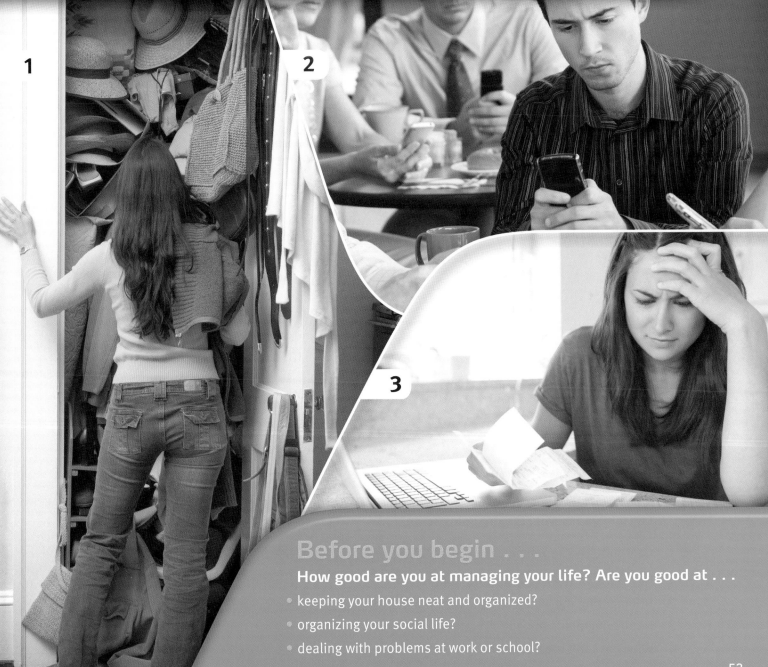

1

2

3

Before you begin . . .

How good are you at managing your life? Are you good at . . .

- keeping your house neat and organized?
- organizing your social life?
- dealing with problems at work or school?

Hello?

• • • • • • • • •

Oh, hi, Brandon. How are you?

• • • • • • • • •

Good, really good. . . . No, it's OK. I'm on my way home.

• • • • • • • •

What am I doing tomorrow night? Actually, I don't think I'm doing anything. . . .

• • • • • • • • •

Oh, wait. Tomorrow's Tuesday. I have my kickboxing class. That starts at 7:00, and then I'm meeting Anna afterwards. We're going to have dinner together. But, yeah, I'd love to catch up with you. How about Wednesday night?

• • • • • • • •

Huh. So you're going to be out of town for a couple of days, . . . but you'll be back Friday, right? So what about Friday?

• • • • • • • •

Uh-oh. I just remembered. My boss is going to have us all work late Friday. She mentioned it last week. We have this big deadline.

• • • • • • • •

Yeah, yeah. We won't be finished on time. It's a long story. Uh, I'll tell you about it sometime.

• • • • • • • •

Tonight? Actually, I'm not doing anything!

• • • • • • • •

That's a fabulous idea. I'll just stop by my apartment to get changed, and then I'll come right over to meet you. I can get there by 7:30. And I'll call for a reservation.

• • • • • • • •

Great. So, see you in about an hour. Bye.

1 Getting started

A What kinds of plans do you make in advance? at the last minute? Tell the class.

B ◀)) 2.20 Listen. Stacy is talking on the phone to her friend Brandon. When do they decide to meet? Can you guess what they're going to do?

Figure it out **C** Complete the sentences. How does Stacy tell Brandon about these things?

1. Her plans with Anna tomorrow night: "We _____ together."

2. Not meeting the work deadline on Friday: "We _____ on time."

3. Not having plans tonight: "I _____ anything."

4. Why she can't meet tomorrow: "I _____ class."

2 Grammar Talking about the future ◀)) 2.21

Extra practice p. 145

Use *will* when you decide to do something as you are speaking.	I'**ll** just stop by my apartment to get changed and then I'**ll** come right over to meet you. (NOT I come right over . . .)
Use *will* or *be going to* for factual information or predictions based on what you know.	You'**re going to** be out of town, but you'll be back Friday? My boss **is going to** make us work late Friday. Our project **won't** be finished on time.
Use the present continuous or *be going to* (not *will*) for decisions you've made and fixed plans.	I'**m meeting** Anna after my kickboxing class. We'**re going to** have dinner together. I'**m not doing** anything tonight.
Use the simple present for schedules.	I **have** my kickboxing class tomorrow. It **starts** at 7:00.

A Complete the conversations with appropriate ways to talk about the future, using the words given. There may be more than one possible answer. Then practice with a partner.

1. A So, what _____ you _____ (do) after class tomorrow?

    B Well, actually, I _____ (take) the afternoon off tomorrow. I _____ (have) lunch with my sister. So yeah, I _____ (not / work) in the afternoon.

    A That sounds nice. Where _____ you _____ (have) lunch?

    B I'm not sure. Do you want to meet us? I'm sure my sister _____ (not / mind).

    A OK. Sure. I _____ (text) you tomorrow when I get out of class.

2. A I _____ (have) a party at my place Friday night. Can you come?

    B Actually, I _____ (have) basketball practice at 7:00 on Friday. It _____ (not finish) until 9:00. Is that too late?

    A No, not at all. My guess is that most people _____ (not arrive) until after 9:00 anyway.

    B OK, great. So I _____ (come) over right after practice. It _____ (be) around 9:30.

3. A So _____ you _____ (go away) this weekend?

    B Actually, we _____ (go) on a boat trip on the lake on Saturday. The weather report says it _____ (not / be) too windy. So yeah, it _____ (be) fun, I think.

    A That sounds great. I've never done that.

    B You're kidding. Why don't you come with us? The boat _____ (leave) at 9:00. I _____ (call) my brother and ask him to get you a ticket.

About you **B** **Pair work** Ask and answer the questions above. Give your own answers.

3 Listening and speaking Fun invitations

A ◀)) 2.22 Listen. Complete the chart. Which invitation sounds the most interesting to you?

	Anton	Clareta	Callie
What's the invitation for?	*a concert*		
What day? What time?			
What are his / her plans then?			
What does he / she decide to do?			

B **Pair work** Student A: Invite your partner to do something with you on a specific day. Student B: Tell your partner your plans for that day, and make a decision about what to do.

1 Building vocabulary and grammar

A 🔊 **2.23** **Read the posts and replies on the website. Complete the expressions with the correct form of *do* or *make*. Then listen and check.**

Ask the LIFE COACH | Do you have a personal problem that you'd rather not discuss with friends or family? Get some confidential advice from our online life coach.

Q1 Sometimes I think I ought to ___*do*___ some **volunteer work** in a school or a hospital, but I'm too busy just trying to _____ **a living**. I have very little free time, so I think I'd better not add anything to my schedule right now. Am I right?

Coach Don't _____ **excuses**. You don't have to spend all your free time doing volunteer work – three hours a week is enough. _____ **some research**, and find an organization where you feel you can _____ **a difference** and _____ **some good** for other people.

Q2 My boss is a bully. He yells at me if I _____ **a mistake**, and he _____ **fun of** me in front of my co-workers. I've tried talking to him, but it doesn't _____ **any good**. He won't listen. I guess I'm going to have to _____ **something** about this problem, but what?

Coach It doesn't _____ **any sense** to ignore this problem, and you'd better do something quickly before it gets worse. _____ **an appointment** with your Human Resources representative. You might want to take a colleague with you, too.

Q3 I'm meeting my girlfriend's parents for the first time next weekend. They've invited me for dinner. I'm going to _____ **my best** to _____ **a good impression** on them, but I'm really nervous. Any advice?

Coach _____ **an effort** to dress nicely, and _____ **sure** you take them a small gift, such as flowers or chocolates. _____ **some nice comments** about their home, the food, etc., but don't overdo it. You ought to let them _____ **the talking** at first. The most important thing, however, is just to be yourself.

Q4 My boss recently offered me a promotion. I've _____ **a lot of thinking** about it, but I can't _____ **up my mind** if I should take it. Sometimes I think I'd rather stay in my current job. I've got to decide by next week. What should I do?

Coach _____ **a list** of the pros and cons of each job, and give each one a score from 1 to 5 (5 = the best). Then _____ **the math** – add up the points for each list, and subtract the con totals from the pro totals. Which job has the highest score? Does that help you _____ **a decision**?

Word sort **B** **Make word webs like these for *do* and *make*. Add other expressions you know. Then discuss the life coach's advice with a partner. Do you agree? What advice can you add?**

some volunteer work

Figure it out **C** **Find expressions on the website with the same meanings as the underlined words below.**

1. I <u>should</u> do some volunteer work.
2. You <u>really should</u> do something quickly.
3. I <u>have to</u> make a decision soon.
4. I'<u>d prefer</u> to stay in the same job.

2 Grammar What's advisable, necessary, preferable ◀)) 2.24

Extra practice p. 145

What's advisable	You'**d better** do something quickly. (*'d = had*) I'**d better not** add anything to my schedule. I **ought to** do some volunteer work. You **ought to** let them do the talking. You **might want to** take a colleague with you.
What's necessary	I'**m going to have to** do something about it. I'**ve got to** decide by next week. (*'ve = have*) You **don't have to** spend time on this.
What's preferable	I'**d rather** (**not**) stay in my current job. (*'d = would*)

In conversation

Should is more common than **ought to** or **had better**.

▬▬▬▬▬ *should*
■ *ought to*
▮ *had better*

✖ Common errors

Don't use *had better* for general advice.

You **shouldn't** ignore problems. (NOT You ~~had better not~~ ignore problems.)

Pair work Complete the conversations with problems and solutions. Then compare with a partner. Did you have any of the same ideas?

1. A   We have a test tomorrow, so I ought to _____ tonight, but I'd rather _____ .
   B   You know, I think you'd better _____ because _____ .

2. A   I don't know what to do. I received an offer for a job. It looks really interesting, but it doesn't pay very well. I'm going to have to make up my mind if I want to _____ .
   B   That's a hard decision to make. You might want to _____ .

3. A   I need more exercise. I ought to make an effort to _____ every day, but it takes so much time.
   B   Well, you don't have to _____ , but you ought to _____ .

4. A   I have a friend who makes fun of me all the time, but I'd rather not _____ .
   B   That's not good. I think you're going to have to _____ .

5. A   My sister hasn't applied to college. She's got to _____ if she wants to _____ .
   B   She'd better decide soon because _____ she's got to _____ .

3 Speaking naturally Reduction of verbs

*You might **want to** try a new instructor. (**wanna**)*   *You **ought to** take more lessons. (**oughta**)*
*You'd **better** study the driver's manual. (**you better**)*   *You'**ve got to** pay attention! (**gotta**)*
*You're **going to have to** practice more. (**gonna hafta**)*

A ◀)) 2.25 Listen and repeat the sentences above. Notice the reduction of the verbs. In what situation might a person give this advice? Can you think of other advice?

About you   **B** **Group work** Think of six pieces of advice for a student who's not doing well in class.

4 Talk about it What's your advice?

Group work Imagine a friend is in each situation. Give as much advice as you can.

1. You're tired and don't feel like going to a friend's party, but you know you ought to go.
2. You have time to do some regular volunteer work on the weekend or take a part-time job.
3. You had an interview for a job you really want, but it didn't go well.

"Well, you ought to just tell your friend, you know. And say you're not in the mood for a party."

(((**Sounds right** p. 138

I've got to get going.

1 Conversation strategy Ending phone conversations

A When was the last time you were running late? Why? Tell the class.

B 🔊 2.26 Listen. Why can't Ling talk longer on the phone?

ASSERTIVENESS
SEMINAR
—
4TH FLOOR

Ramon Hi, Ling. It's Ramon. Is this a good time to talk?

Ling Um, not really. I'm late for a seminar. I'm going to have to run.

Ramon Oh, OK. I just wanted to ask about this weekend.

Ling Well, can I call you back tonight? I've got to get going.

Ramon OK. I'll be home after 8:00. I'm going to the gym after work.

Ling Oh, good. I'll call you later. I'd better go now.

Ramon Yeah. So think about what you want to do on Saturday.

Ling Yeah, I will. Listen, Ramon, I've really got to go. I'm already late.

Ramon All right. I'll let you go. By the way, what's your seminar about?

Ling Being assertive. Bye now!

Ramon Oh, OK! Talk to you later.

C **Notice** how Ling tries to end the phone conversation with expressions like these. Find examples in the conversation.

I'd better go.	*Can I call you back?*
I've got to get going.	*I'll call you later.*
I'm going to have to run.	*I've really got to go.*

D **Pair work** Practice the phone conversation below six times. Think of a new excuse, and use a different expression to end the conversation each time.

> Hi, _____ (name). Is this a good time to talk?

> Not really. I'm just cooking dinner. (Give an excuse) Can I call you back? (Use an expression)

2 Strategy plus   Friendly good-byes

In friendly or informal phone conversations, you can use short expressions like these to say *good-bye*. The words in parentheses are usually dropped.

(I'll) Talk to you later.
(I'll) Catch you later.
(I'll) See you later.
I('ve) got to go. / (I've) Got to go.
I('d) better go.
(It was) Nice talking to you.

Talk to you later.

In conversation

The shorter forms of these expressions are more common.

See you later.
I'll / We'll see you later.
Talk to you later.
I'll / We'll talk to you later.

Write the shorter forms of the underlined expressions to make these conversations more informal. Then practice the conversations with a partner.

1. A Hi, it's me. Are you on your way?
   B Yeah. I'll be there in about half an hour.
   A All right. <u>I'll see you soon</u>.
2. A Well, my appointment is at 2:00, so <u>I'd better go</u>.
   B OK. <u>I'll talk to you later</u>.
   A Yeah. <u>I've got to go</u>. <u>I'll see you later</u>.
3. A OK, well, <u>I'd better let you go</u>.
   B Yeah. <u>It was nice talking to you</u>.
   A Yeah. Take care. Bye.
4. A Listen, my train's coming. <u>I'll catch you later</u>.
   B Yeah. <u>I'll see you tomorrow</u>. Bye.

3 Strategies   Role-play phone conversations

Pair work Student A: Choose a topic below. Call your partner. Try to keep the conversation going.
Student B: Try to end the conversation. Then change roles.

- plans for the weekend
- how your week is going
- something you're looking forward to
- something you want to borrow
- some exciting news
- something you're busy with

A *Hey, Rick. How are things going?*
B *Not bad. Busy. Actually, I have an appointment at the dentist at 2:00. Can I call you back?*
A *Well, I was just calling about my band. We need someone to make a flyer for us.*

Free talk p. 132

1 Reading

A Do you ever multitask? What kinds of things do you do at the same time? Is multitasking a good thing to do?

B Read the blog. What does it say about multitasking?

http://www.theartandscienceof...

The Art (and Science) of Doing Less and Achieving More

"To do two things at once is to do neither." – Publilius Syrus, Roman philosopher, 100 BCE

Multitasking: An Effective Solution?

With the introduction of various technologies into our everyday lives, multitasking has become a normal feature of our busy days. Doing more tasks ought to mean that we get more done. But does it really? Take this example from a typical day at my job.

Last week, during a meeting, I decided to send a quick email to a client. A minute later, I had to send another email with the attachment I had forgotten. In my third email to him, I had to apologize for sending the *wrong* attachment. When I eventually focused on the meeting, I realized someone was asking me a question, but because I wasn't paying attention, I couldn't answer it and I had to ask him to repeat it. Embarrassing.

Sound familiar? Don't worry – you're not alone. Research shows that when we multitask, we are actually playing a trick on ourselves. We *think* we're doing more, but actually we're not. In fact, multitasking can lead to a 40 percent drop in productivity. Researchers say that we don't really multitask at all; we "switch-task," and when we switch from one thing to another, we're simply interrupting ourselves to do something else.

An Alternative Approach

I did some thinking about all of this and decided to do some research for myself. For one week, I would make an effort *not* to multitask. During that week, I discovered two surprising things.

First, I made great progress on challenging projects. I stayed with each project when it got hard, and it really made a difference. Now, I no longer avoid tough assignments, I don't get distracted by other things, and I finish one job before I go on to another – even if the job is driving me crazy!

Second, my stress levels dropped dramatically. Research shows that multitasking isn't just inefficient, it's stressful, and I found that was true. It was actually a relief to finish one thing before going on to the next. So how can we change our multi-tasking ways?

A Cure for Multitaskers

First, get rid of interruptions. I now know that when I'm working, I should resist the temptation to check email, and I make sure my phone is turned off.

Second, set yourself a tight deadline. If you think you have to give a presentation in 30 minutes, you might not want to answer that interrupting phone call! Single-tasking to meet a tight deadline will also reduce your stress levels – as long as you meet it, of course!

My experiment convinced me that I don't have to accept multitasking as a way of life. If you make up your mind to avoid distractions and concentrate on one job at a time, you really can achieve more.

^{About you} **C** Replace the underlined words in each question with the correct form of an expression from the blog. Then ask and answer the questions with a partner.

1. Have you ever <u>done something to fool</u> someone? How did it turn out?
2. What do you do if you're not <u>moving forward on</u> an assignment?
3. Do you often <u>have your attention interrupted by</u> email or phone calls?
4. What kinds of personality traits <u>annoy you a lot</u>?
5. Do you ever <u>decide on a time to finish something that's hard to achieve</u>?
6. Do you find it easy to <u>make decisions</u> about things?

D Read the blog again. Answer the questions. Then compare your answers with a partner.

1. What happened when the writer tried to multitask?
2. What was the research the writer did?
3. What were the two things the writer learned?
4. What two things does the writer recommend we do to stop multitasking?
5. What is the writer's opinion of multitasking? Do you agree?

2 **Listening and writing** When should I do that?

^{About you} **A** What do you do when you have a lot to do? How do you balance work, friends, and family time?

B 🔊 **2.27** Listen to four people talk about their time management problems. Which problems did they have? Write the number of the speaker. There are two extra problems.

a. I left things until the last minute. _____
b. I couldn't set priorities. _____
c. I felt I had too much to do. _____
d. I couldn't meet deadlines. _____
e. I took on too many jobs. _____
f. I delayed difficult jobs. _____

C 🔊 **2.27** Listen again and write the advice each speaker received.

D Read the Help note. Then read the question and answer and circle any sentences that link ideas with *as long as*, *provided that*, or *unless*.

I'm trying to be more organized, so I decided to record my lectures, but I never have time to watch them. Any ideas?

Unless you find time to watch the recordings, there is really no point in having them. So make time to review them – provided that they are worth watching again, of course!
Most people waste time when they are traveling to and from work or school, so use that time to watch your classes on your laptop – as long as you're not driving, of course!

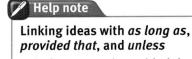
Help note

Linking ideas with *as long as*, *provided that*, and *unless*
- *As long as* and *provided that* mean "if" or "only if."
- *Unless* means "except if" or "if . . . not."

^{About you} **E** **Pair work** Write a question about a time management problem. Then exchange papers and answer your classmate's question. Give advice.

Learning tip *Writing sentences to show meaning*

When you learn a new expression, use it in a sentence to help you remember it. Add another sentence to clarify or paraphrase the meaning.

My brother can't make a living as a musician. He doesn't earn enough money.

1 Complete the sentences with these expressions.

| do my best | make a difference | make a good impression | make up my mind |

1. I'm going to try to _____ on my new boss. I want her to have a good opinion of me.
2. I'd like to do something useful in life. I want to _____ in people's lives.
3. I can't _____ if I want to buy a new cell phone. I can't decide if I need one.
4. I find exams very stressful, but I always _____. I try very hard to do well.

2 Write sentences to help you remember these expressions.

| do some thinking | do volunteer work | make an effort |
| do something fun | make a decision | make fun of someone |

3 Word builder Which expressions below can you complete with *make*? Find appropriate verbs to complete the other expressions. Write the words on the lines.

1. _____ changes
2. _____ a mess
3. _____ a dream
4. _____ progress
5. _____ a suggestion
6. _____ plans
7. _____ a walk
8. _____ a favor

On your own

Choose five expressions and make a "to do" list using them.

Can Do! Now I can . . .

| ✓ I can . . . | ? I need to review how to . . . |

- [ ] talk about the future.
- [ ] ask for and give advice about personal situations.
- [ ] end phone calls with expressions like *I'd better go.*
- [ ] say good-bye in a friendly, informal way.
- [ ] understand people discussing invitations.
- [ ] understand people discussing time management.
- [ ] read a blog about multitasking.
- [ ] write some advice about time management.

1 What do you think?

A Complete these opinions with a verb or *to* + verb. Compare with a partner.

1. Parents shouldn't let teenagers __*watch*__ violent shows on TV.
2. Parents ought to make their kids _____ books every night.
3. Teachers ask students _____ too much homework.
4. Parents shouldn't help their children _____ their homework.
5. Parents shouldn't let their children _____ too much junk food.
6. Parents should get their kids _____ more vegetables and fewer sweets.
7. We shouldn't let young people _____ cars until they're 21.
8. We ought to make all teenagers _____ some volunteer work.

B **Group work** Discuss three or four opinions above. Use the expressions in the boxes to give your opinions and to show when you agree.

A If you ask me, parents shouldn't let teenagers watch violent shows on TV.

B Absolutely. It seems to me that teenagers are becoming more violent because of TV.

C I don't know. I don't think people learn violent behavior from TV.

i Give an opinion

If you ask me, . . .
It seems to me that . . .
I don't think . . .

i Agree

Definitely.
Absolutely.
You're right.
That's for sure.

2 The way it used to be

Complete the story with the correct form of the verbs below.

be	bring	buy	complain	get	hate	live	play	push	✓ visit

When I was a kid, we used to __*visit*__ my grandparents every month. They _____ two hours from our home, so we always _____ some books to read in the car. I used to _____ the drive, and I'd always _____ , so my dad would _____ us ice cream. That _____ fun. When we _____ to my grandparents' house, my grandma would always let us _____ in her yard. They had a swing set, and my grandpa would _____ us on the swings.

3 How many words can you remember?

Write expressions with *do* or *make* about six family members or friends. Then tell a partner about each person, using the expressions.

1. my uncle George > makes his living as a teacher / doesn't make a lot of money
2. my friend Yoko > does medical research

"My uncle George makes his living as a teacher. He doesn't make a lot of money, but he loves his work."

4 What's going to happen?

Complete the conversation with appropriate ways to talk about the future, using the verbs given. More than one correct answer is possible in some cases. Then practice with a partner.

Cindy What time does your train __leave__ (leave) today?

Dana I _____ (take) the 3:30 train. Oh, no, it's almost 3:00!

Cindy Don't worry. I _____ (drive) you to the station.

Dana Oh, you don't have to do that. I _____ (call) a taxi.

Cindy No way! I can take you. I _____ (go) to the mall this afternoon. It's not far from the train station.

Dana Are you sure it _____ (not be) a problem?

Cindy No problem at all. I _____ (meet) a friend there at 4:00.

Dana Well, OK. Thanks. I _____ (get) my suitcase.

Cindy Yeah. We _____ (have to) leave right away.

Dana OK. I _____ (be) ready in five minutes.

5 A healthy diet?

A Complete the sentences with different foods. Use your own ideas. Then discuss with a partner. Do you agree?

1. It's not healthy to eat too many __hamburgers__ .
2. If you want to lose weight, eat very few _____ .
3. If you eat too much _____ , you'll gain weight.
4. You should drink very little _____ .
5. A little _____ every day is good for you.
6. People should eat less _____ and more _____ .

B **Pair work** Replace the underlined words in these sentences. How many true sentences can you make? Compare with a partner.

1. I like boiled eggs better than fried eggs.
2. I drink about three cans of soda a day.
3. I'm trying to eat less ice cream and fewer doughnuts.
4. I always keep a jar of mayonnaise in my refrigerator.
5. I ate too much candy and not enough fruit yesterday.

   A I like roast chicken better than fried chicken. How about you?
   B Actually, I prefer barbecued chicken.

6 Get off the phone!

Role play Student A: You are planning a special dinner for an English-speaking visitor to your country. Call your partner to ask for advice about what kind of food to prepare.

Student B: Your partner calls to ask for advice just as you are leaving to meet a friend. Try to end the conversation politely.

UNIT 1 What are we like?

1 Class activity What new things can you find out about your classmates?
Ask questions and take notes.

Find someone who . . .	Name	Notes
eats extremely slowly.	Kenji	Friends say, "Hurry up."
reads very fast.		
gets impatient easily.		
is incredibly organized.		
can do math in his or her head quickly.		
thinks it's important to dress properly.		
automatically turns on the TV when he or she gets home.		
plays several sports really well.		
remembers dates and numbers very easily.		
likes to do things absolutely perfectly.		

"So do you eat extremely slowly?"   *"Yes, I do. My friends are always saying 'Hurry up.'"*

2 Class work Tell the class something new and interesting that you learned about two classmates.

UNIT 2 I've never done that!

1 Are there things you've *never* done that you think people in your group *have* done? Complete the
chart with things that you have *never* done. Try to think of surprising things.

Think of . . .	I've never . . .	Points
a sport you've never done.	I've never been snowboarding.	2
a tourist attraction in your town or city you've never visited.		
something you've never understood.		
a food you've never eaten.		
a well-known movie you've never seen.		
a TV show you've never watched.		
something you've never drunk.		
something else you've never done.		
	Total points	

2 Group game Now ask your classmates questions. Score a point for every person who *has* done
the thing you haven't done. The person with the most points wins.

A I've never been snowboarding. Have you?
B Yeah. I've been snowboarding a lot. I love it.

C Me too!
A OK. So, that gives me two points

129

UNIT **3** ## Where's the best place to . . . ?

1 **Pair work** What advice would you give to someone visiting your country for the first time? Discuss the categories below, and agree on one idea for each category.

MY COUNTRY ### ADVICE FOR FIRST-TIME VISITORS

The most famous attraction

The most beautiful natural feature

The cheapest way to travel around the country

The most comfortable place to stay

The best souvenir

The nicest shopping area

The most unusual food to try

The worst thing to do

The city with the most things to see

The most interesting thing to do in the evening

The least interesting place to visit

A *Well, everyone should go see Tokyo Sky Tree. It's probably the most famous attraction. It's definitely popular.*

B *It sure is. But what about Osaka Castle?*

2 **Group work** Join another pair. Compare your ideas. Did you have any of the same ideas?

UNIT 4 Family histories

1 Prepare a short history of your family. Use these ideas to help you.

Think about . . .

- where your grandparents are from.
- interesting facts about your aunts and uncles.
- how your parents met.
- where your parents used to live when they were younger.
- how your family life has changed.
- any special memories you have.

_____

_____

_____

_____

2 **Group work** Present your family history to the group. Listen to your classmates' histories. Take notes, and ask them questions for more information.

"My father's parents are from Guadalajara. They moved to Mexico City in 1965. My father grew up there. . . . My mother's parents . . . "

UNIT 5 Whichever is easier

1 **Group work** Imagine you and your classmates are going to have a "potluck" dinner tonight. Everyone must bring food – but only what you already have at home. Decide on the following:

1. Are you going to go to someone's home? Whose?
2. What time do you want to arrive?
3. Do you have enough plates?
4. Do you need to bring silverware (knives, forks, spoons, etc.)? Do you have enough?
5. What drinks are you going to have?
6. What dishes do you want to cook?
7. What food does each person need to bring?
8. Is someone going to bring music?
9. Are you going to play any games?

   A *Well, there are five of us. The table in my apartment isn't big enough, but we could sit on the floor.*

   B *Why don't we eat at the park?*

   A *Either way for me. How about you, Melly?*

2 **Class activity** Tell the class about your potluck dinner. Decide which dinner you would like to go to. Which is the most popular?

6 Who's going to do what?

ℹ **Useful language**

I'd rather (not) . . .

I'd prefer to . . .

It seems to me that . . .

Should we . . . ?

We might want to . . .

We're going to have to take . . .

We'd better (not) . . . because . . .

We ought to . . .

Where / When are we going to . . . ?

Who's going to . . . ?

1 Group work Imagine you are going to hold a community event in your school or neighborhood. The event should have a theme, food, and entertainment.

Discuss the following:

1. When is the event going to be? Where? What time?
2. What theme will the event have? (for example, a holiday theme, a "green" theme?)
3. What kinds of attractions or entertainment will you have at the event?
4. How much will it cost to run the event?
5. What are you going to do to get ready for the event? Who's going to do what?

A *Well, we ought to hold the event right away because the weather's good.*

B *I agree, though we might want to wait a month – there's a lot to prepare.*

2 Class activity Take turns telling the class about your event. After you have heard about all the events, vote on the one that you'd like to go to. Which event do most people want to go to?

UNIT **1** 🔊 4.30 **Listen and repeat the words. Is the stress in each word like the stress in** *fairly, admire,* *arrogant,* **or** *correctly*? **Write the words from the list in the correct columns below.**

1. complain
2. dishonest
3. forget
4. generous
5. helpful
6. impatient
7. reckless
8. wonderful
9. borrow
10. politely
11. relaxed
12. patiently

● · fairly	· ● admire	● · · arrogant	· ● · correctly
	complain		

UNIT **2** 🔊 4.31 **Listen and repeat the words. Notice the different ways the letter** *o* **is pronounced.** **Match the words with the same underlined sounds.**

1. d<u>o</u> _____
2. d<u>o</u>ne _____
3. g<u>o</u> _____
4. g<u>o</u>tten _____

a. forg<u>o</u>t
b. l<u>o</u>se
c. sp<u>o</u>ken
d. w<u>o</u>n

UNIT **3** 🔊 4.32 **Listen and repeat the words. Notice the underlined sounds.** **Which sound in each group is different? Circle the odd one out.**

1. h<u>igh</u> <u>i</u>sland r<u>i</u>ver w<u>i</u>de
2. c<u>o</u>ntinent m<u>o</u>st <u>o</u>cean volcan<u>o</u>
3. airp<u>or</u>t sp<u>or</u>ts st<u>or</u>e w<u>or</u>st
4. ab<u>ou</u>t c<u>ou</u>ntry m<u>ou</u>ntain s<u>ou</u>th
5. b<u>ea</u>ch d<u>ee</u>p m<u>e</u>ter <u>o</u>c<u>ea</u>n

UNIT **4** 🔊 4.33 **Listen and repeat the words. Notice the underlined sounds. Are the sounds like the sounds** **in** *clean, great, law, uncle,* **or** *wife*? **Write the words from the list in the correct columns below.** **There is one extra word.**

1. c<u>ou</u>sin 2. d<u>au</u>ghter 3. f<u>igh</u>t 4. n<u>ie</u>ce 5. n<u>e</u>phew 6. st<u>ay</u>

cl<u>ea</u>n	gr<u>ea</u>t	l<u>aw</u>	<u>u</u>ncle	w<u>i</u>fe
			cousin	

Sounds right

🔊 **4.34** Listen and repeat the pairs of words. Notice the underlined sounds. Are the sounds the same (S) or different (D)? Write *S* or *D*.

1. th**ir**sty / dess**er**t ___S___
2. r**aw** / s**au**ce _____
3. br**o**ccoli / b**oi**led _____
4. fr**ie**s / p**ie** _____
5. sh**ou**ld / p**ou**nd _____
6. t**oo** / s**ou**p _____
7. g**oo**d / f**oo**d _____
8. m**u**ch / l**o**ve _____
9. f**u**ll / h**u**ngry _____

UNIT 6

🔊 **4.35** Listen and repeat the words. Notice the underlined sounds. Are the sounds like the sounds in *h**o**me*, *g**oo**d*, *m**a**th*, *w**or**se*, or *ought*? Write the words from the list in the correct columns below.

1. b**ou**ght
2. b**u**lly
3. t**o**tal
4. f**a**bulous
5. g**ir**lfriend
6. r**a**ther
7. rese**ar**ch
8. sh**ou**ld
9. th**ough**t
10. c**oa**ch

h**o**me	g**oo**d	m**a**th	w**or**se	**ought**
				bought

Extra practice

Lesson A Adjectives vs. manner adverbs

A Choose the correct words to complete the sentences.

1. I know this sounds **bad** / **badly**, but I love to drive really **quick** / **fast**. I think I drive really **good** / **well**, though. I don't get **reckless** / **recklessly** when I get behind the wheel or anything.

2. I try **hard** / **hardly** to be neat and tidy. Like, I always put my keys on the shelf **automatic** / **automatically** when I get home. You can lose your keys so **easy** / **easily**.

3. I think it's **important** / **importantly** to take work **serious** / **seriously**. I mean, it only seems right. If you do a job **good** / **well** you feel **good** / **well** about yourself, too.

4. I guess I can get **impatient** / **impatiently** sometimes. Like, I want **instant** / **instantly** replies to my texts and emails. I just don't like to wait when I need an answer **quick** / **quickly**.

5. I love sports, but I don't really play for fun. I feel pretty **strong** / **strongly** that you should play to win. I feel **terrible** / **terribly** if I lose. My friends see things **different** / **differently** and say that I'm too **serious** / **seriously** about sports and that I should relax.

6. I hate it when people don't write texts **proper** / **properly** and don't use **correct** / **correctly** grammar and punctuation. It's not because they're writing **quick** / **quickly** – they just don't care about it. I always check over my texts very **careful** / **carefully** before I send them.

 B **Pair work** Are any of the sentences above true for you or someone you know? Tell your partner.

Lesson B Adverbs before adjectives and adverbs

A Complete the statements about people's personalities with words from the box.

absolutely crazy	extremely talented	pretty laid-back
arrogant at all	incredibly generous	really reliable

1. My sister's _____ . She's just good at everything she does.

2. My brother's _____ . He does that extreme biking thing, jumping upside down on his bike and everything.

3. My parents are _____ . They bought me a new car when my old one broke down.

4. My best friend is _____ . I can count on her for absolutely anything.

5. I'm _____ . I don't get stressed very often.

6. My brother isn't _____ . He doesn't think he's better than everyone else.

> **X Common errors**
>
> Don't use *very* with extreme adjectives like *wonderful*.
>
> She's **absolutely** wonderful. (NOT She's ~~very~~ wonderful.)

B **Pair work** Make sentences like the ones above about people you know. Tell your partner.

2 Lesson A Present perfect statements

A Use the underlined words to write sentences about travel experiences. Use the present perfect.

1. I / always / do a lot of traveling. I guess it / always / be my main interest in life.
    I've always done a lot of traveling. I guess it's always been my main interest in life.

2. I travel with an old school friend and she / be to lots of places.
    _____

3. She and I / travel around Asia three or four times. We / always / enjoy traveling together.
    _____

4. We / walk on the Great Wall of China twice. It's so amazing.
    _____

5. We / be so lucky. We / visit some amazing places and I / try all kinds of food.
    _____

6. We're always talking about places we would like to go. We / think about going to Australia or India.
    _____

7. My friend / not be to India because she / not have the chance, and I / never be to Australia.
    _____

8. We / not make a decision about where to go next, but I'd really like to go to Sydney.
    _____

About you **B Pair work** Tell a partner five true things about travel. Use the sentences above to help you.

UNIT
2 Lesson B Present perfect vs. simple past

A Complete the conversations about unusual experiences. Use the present perfect or simple past.

1. A *Have you ever done* (you / ever / do) anything scary?
    B Yes, I _____ . I _____ (play) the piano in a big concert last year.
    A Really? _____ (you / play) a solo?
    B No, I _____ . Thank goodness! There _____ (be) an orchestra, too.

2. A _____ (you / ever / see) the Northern Lights?
    B No, I _____ , but I _____ (always / want) to see them. We _____ (go)
       to Alaska last year, but we _____ (not / see) them.

3. A _____ (you / ever / try) kickboxing?
    B Yes, I _____ . I _____ (take) a class last semester. But I _____ (not / like) it.

4. A _____ (you / ever / cook) a meal for a big group of people?
    B Yes, I _____ . It _____ (be) my sister's birthday last weekend.
       She _____ (invite) 25 of her friends, and we _____ (make) Moroccan food.
    A Really? I _____ (never / eat) Moroccan food before. _____ (it / be) good?
    B Oh, yeah. Everybody _____ (love) it!

About you **B Pair work** Ask and answer the questions above. Give your own answers.

Extra practice

3 Lesson A Superlatives

> **✕ Common errors**
>
> Don't use *most* before a superlative that ends in -*est*.
>
> What's **the fastest** way to travel?
> (NOT What's the ~~most fastest~~ way to travel?)

A Complete the facts and tips about different places in the world. Use the superlative forms of the adjectives or *the most / the least* with the nouns.

1. _____ (big) national park in the world is in Greenland.
2. _____ (fast) roller coaster in Europe is in Spain.
3. Canada has _____ (long) coastline in the world. It's great for sightseeing.
4. _____ (expensive) hotel in the world is in Dubai. The rooms cost over $10,000 a night.
5. _____ (good) time to visit Thailand is from November to February. These are the months with _____ (good) weather because there is _____ (rain).
6. Summer is _____ (bad) time to visit Venice because that's when there are _____ (tourists).
7. The city that has _____ (people) in the United States is New York City.
8. The city with _____ (large) population in the world is Shanghai.
9. _____ (deep) lake in the world is Lake Baikal in Siberia.
10. _____ (small) country in the world is Vatican City in Rome. It's also _____ populated country with only 500 inhabitants.

About you **B** **Pair work** Can you think of similar facts and tips for visitors to your country?

3 Lesson B Questions with *How* + adjective . . . ?

A Complete the questions and answers about Spain. Use the words from the box. If you don't need a word to complete the answers, write a dash (–). Some words are used more than once.

big	deep	high	hot	long

1. Q: How _____ is Mount Teide in Tenerife, Spain?
   A: It's 4,964 meters (16,286 feet) _____ .
2. Q: How _____ is the coastline?
   A: It's 7,517 kilometers (4,671 miles) _____ .
3. Q: How _____ is the population of Spain?
   A: It's almost 47 million people _____ .
4. Q: What is the largest natural lake in Spain? How _____ is it?
   A: Lake Sanabria is 51 meters (167 feet) _____ .
5. Q: How _____ is it in southern Spain in August?
   A: It is usually around 35°C (90°F) _____ .

About you **B** **Pair work** What do you know about *your* country? Take turns asking questions similar to the ones above. Do you know the answers?

A OK. So how high is Mount Aconcagua?
B Well, I'm guessing, but I think it's almost 7,000 meters (23,000 feet) high.

UNIT **4** **Lesson A** Verbs *let, make, help, have, get, want, ask, tell*

A Complete the sentences. Use the correct forms of the verbs given.
Sometimes there is more than one correct answer.

1. I want my children _____ (make) good decisions for themselves.
2. I don't let my kids _____ (play) computer games before bedtime.
   It makes them _____ (sleep) badly.
3. I usually make my teenagers _____ (clean up) the kitchen after meals.
4. I want to get my kids _____ (eat) well. They're always eating junk food.
5. I usually tell my kids _____ (do) their homework before dinner, but I don't help
   them _____ (do) it.
6. I'm always asking them _____ (turn off) the lights in the house.
7. I have them _____ (shut down) their computers at night.
8. I'm always telling my kids _____ (be) careful when they go out.
9. I always have my kids _____ (write) thank-you letters when they get a gift.
10. We often help our sons _____ (study) for exams. We make up games for them.

About you **B** **Pair work** Read the sentences above again. Did your parents say similar
things about you when you were growing up? Discuss with a partner.

"My parents wanted me to do well in school. They made me study every night."

UNIT **4** **Lesson B** *used to* and *would*

A Read this person's memories about her summer vacations. Rewrite eight sentences using *used to*
or *would*. Sometimes both are correct.

When I was younger, we had long school vacations in the summer – about 10 weeks. I saw a lot of
my extended family in those days. They lived about 30 miles away. My cousins came to stay
every summer. We didn't have a big house like we do now, so we always camped in the backyard.
There was a stream near our house, and we swam in it. One of my little cousins didn't like
swimming. She was really scared of water, and my brother always teased her about it. He made her
go into the water. He wasn't very nice to her. Thank goodness he's not like that now!

_____

_____

_____

_____

_____

_____

About you **B** **Pair work** Ask and answer questions about your elementary school summer breaks, using
Did you use to . . . ?

A *Did you use to spend your summers with your family?*
B *Not really. I used to play with the kids in the neighborhood. We'd go off and . . .*

143

Extra practice

UNIT **5** **Lesson A** Talking about quantities of food

A Complete the sentences about shopping and eating habits. Use the words in the box.

a few	cartons	few	fewer	less	less	little	loaves	many

1. I don't eat _____ fruits or vegetables. I really should eat more healthy food.
2. We have a small freezer so we buy very _____ frozen meals.
3. I prefer to go shopping at the local store. I'm trying to buy _____ food from the big supermarkets than I used to.
4. My family buys about six _____ of bread a week and eight _____ of fruit juice.
5. I don't fry food anymore. It means I eat _____ calories and _____ fat. But I have to say, I like a _____ butter on my potatoes.
6. When I go out to eat, I like to try _____ different things that I don't normally eat.

About you **B** **Pair work** Are any of the sentences above true for you? What other shopping and eating habits do you have?

UNIT **5** **Lesson B** *too, too much, too many,* and *enough*

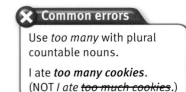

Common errors

Use *too many* with plural countable nouns.

I ate *too many cookies*.
(NOT I ate ~~too much cookies~~.)

A Complete the online forum conversation with *too, too many, too much,* and *enough.*

A few months ago, I completely changed my eating habits. I used to eat ___*too much*___ sugar, _____ processed fat, and _____ take-out meals. I also didn't eat my meals slowly _____ because I was always rushing out somewhere. My mother was always saying 'You eat _____ quickly.' or 'You're not eating _____ protein,' and as for fast food, I know I definitely ate _____ . I really thought my mom complained _____ , but actually I guess I didn't pay _____ attention to her. I got sick! The doctor said my diet wasn't healthy _____ and said I needed to change it. He also told me that I needed more vitamins and that I wasn't getting _____ . No surprise there! So I changed my diet. In the end, it was simple _____ to do. Now I'm eating a lot of raw vegetables – I guess you can't eat _____ of those! I feel great. And guess what? My mom can't say I don't eat well _____ . Not now!

COMMENTS:

Good for you! You should never be _____ busy to look after your health! _____ junk food and _____ sweets are not good for you.

About you **B** Write your own comment to add to the forum. Then compare with a partner.

"I eat very little healthy food, too. I guess I should eat less fast food."

144

UNIT 6

Lesson A Talking about the future

A A man is telling a friend about his plans for the evening. Circle the correct phrases to complete the sentences. Sometimes both are correct.

Well, tonight (**I'm going to stop** / **I stop**) by the store on my way home. I need to get some stuff for dinner. I think **I'll buy** / **I'm buying** some pasta, and **I'll make** / **I make** some garlic bread. That sounds good. So, yeah, **we eat** / **we're eating** late tonight because **I have** / **I'll have** a gym class at 6:00. I think **I'll go** / **I'm going to go** home straight after class, because **my roommate's having** / **my roommate has** dinner with me tonight. I guess **he's not getting** / **he won't get** home until 7:30, so maybe **we'll eat** / **we're eating** at about 8:00. I think **we're going to go** / **we go** out later. There's a movie I want to see. It **starts** / **will start** at 10:00.

About you **B** **Pair work** What plans do you have for tonight? Tell your partner.

UNIT 6

Lesson B What's *advisable, necessary, preferable*

A Rewrite these sentences about making changes in life. Use the words given.

> **Common errors**
>
> Use *have to*, not *'d better*, for general advice. Use *'d better* for a particular situation.
>
> ***You have to get*** *a visa to travel to some countries.* (NOT ~~*You'd better get*~~ *a visa to travel to some countries.*)

1. I'd prefer not to move out of my apartment. ('d rather not)
    I'd rather not move out of my apartment.

2. I should really learn to drive. (be going to have to)
    _____

3. I should save some money to buy a car. (ought to)
    _____

4. I think you should talk to your boss about a promotion. (might want to)
    _____

5. My brother should get a job soon, or he won't be able to pay his rent. (had better)
    _____

6. My classmates shouldn't go out tonight, or they won't pass the exam tomorrow. (had better not)
    _____

7. My sister wants to go to Europe. She should learn some English before she goes. ('d better)
    _____

8. My friend has to choose her major soon, but she says she prefers not to think about it. ('d rather not)
    _____

9. My parents are going to have to retire soon, but they say they prefer to work. (would rather)
    _____

10. I should get more exercise – I spend too much time at my desk. (ought to)
    _____

About you **B** **Pair work** Make the sentences you wrote true for you. Then compare.

"I'd rather not stay in my apartment. It's too small!"

145

Illustration credits

Photography credits

Text credits

Answers

Unit 3, Lesson A

1 Getting started, Exercise B, page 22

1. b Taipei. Taipei 101 is the tallest office building in the world.
2. a Japan. The Akashi-Kaikyo Bridge is the longest suspension bridge.
3. b China. The New South China Mall is the largest shopping mall.
4. b Moscow. McDonald's is the world's busiest restaurant.
5. c Barcelona. Camp Nou is the largest soccer stadium in Europe.
6. c France.

1 Getting started, Exercise C, page 22

1. What's the <u>biggest</u> train station in the world?
    Grand Central Station in New York City. It has the most platforms.
2. What's the <u>busiest</u> airport in the world?
    Harsfield-Jackson Atlanta International Airport in Georgia, U.S.A. It has the most passengers.
3. Where is the <u>largest</u> building in the world?
    Boeing Everett Factory in Washington, U.S.A. It has the most usable space.
4. What's the <u>most expensive</u> city in the world?
    Tokyo.